Sweet Panic

A child psychologist's understanding of contemporary life is brought into question when she finds herself stalked by the mother of one of her young clients. Casting an acute eye over the changing face of urban life, Stephen Poliakoff's vibrant and compelling new play pits the two women against each other in a battle for the soul of the city.

Stephen Poliakoff, born in 1952, was appointed Writer in Residence at the National Theatre for 1976 and the same year won the Evening Standard's Most Promising Playwright award for *Hitting Town* and *City Sugar*. He has also won a BAFTA award for the Best Single Play of 1980 for *Caught on a Train*, and the Evening Standard Best British Film award for *Close My Eyes* in 1992. His plays and films include *Clever Soldiers* (1974), *The Carnation Gang* (1974), *Hitting Town* (1975), *City Sugar* (1975), *Heroes* (1975), *Strawberry Fields* (1977), *Stronger than the Sun* (1977), *Shout Across the River* (1978), *American Days* (1979), *The Summer Party* (1980), *Bloody Kids* (1980), *Caught on a Train* (1980), *Favourite Nights* (1981), *Soft Targets* (1982), *Runners* (1983), *Breaking the Silence* (1984), *Coming in to Land* (1987), *Hidden City* (1988), *She's Been Away* (1989), *Playing with Trains* (1989), *Close My Eyes* (1991), *Sienna Red* (1992) and *Century* (1994).

For a complete catalogue of Methuen Drama titles write to:

Methuen Drama
Michelin House
81 Fulham Road
London SW3 6RB

DILLO
£ 7.99

Stephen Poliakoff

Sweet Panic

Methuen Drama

A Methuen Fast Track Playscript

First published in Great Britain in 1996
by Methuen Drama
an imprint of Reed International Books Ltd
Michelin House, 81 Fulham Road, London SW3 6RB
and Auckland, Melbourne, Singapore and Toronto
and distributed in the United States of America
by Heinemann, a division of Reed Elsevier Inc.
361 Hanover Street, Portsmouth, New Hampshire
NH 03801 3959

ISBN 0 413 70750 4

A CIP catalogue record for this book is available from the
British Library

Typeset by Wilmaset Ltd, Birkenhead, Wirral
Printed in Great Britain by Cox & Wyman Ltd, Reading,
Berkshire

Sweet Panic

Sweet Panic was first performed at the Hampstead Theatre, London, on 1 February 1996. The cast was as follows:

Clare	Harriet Walter
Mrs Trevel	Saskia Reeves
Martin	Mark Tandy
Richard	Rupert Penry-Jones
Gina	Kate Isitt
Mr Boulton	Philip Bird

Directed by Stephen Poliakoff
Designed by Tom Piper
Lighting by David Hersey
Sound by John A. Leonard

The time is the present.

Act One

Scene One

The set not cluttered, part a sense of a room, part a sense of the city. London. **Clare** *is in her late thirties. Alone on stage unrolling a chewing-gum packet. She takes out the chewing-gum but does not yet put it in her mouth. She looks up at us.*

Clare Leo is twelve. He comes to see me once a week. He is intelligent, always goes to school, always on time – but then does his best to ruin any class he's in. He specialises in singing obscene versions of television theme tunes.

She sits, stretches out her legs and stares at her shoes. Rather elegant shoes.

He's very proud of his sneakers. Which in fact aren't like any sneakers I've seen. Dyed a strange purple.

She starts chewing the gum, and becomes Leo. Conveying the essence of a feisty twelve-year-old without doing a totally direct impersonation.

(*As Leo*) It's the worst that could happen. My mum and dad are taking me on holiday for a week. It's the worst because whatever happens they'll make out we had a really WICKED time – that's what they think I say when I'm pleased. They'll make out it was great . . . and *you* know what's going to happen . . . *you* know how it'll be.

She takes out the chewing-gum and sticks it carefully on some surface. Leo's father, **Mr Boulton***, comes on and sits in a chair opposite her, a small table between them.*

Boulton It was good, it was fine . . . travelling through France without incident. We had a very good time, we survived.

Clare (*calmly*) Survived, or had a good time?

Boulton It was excellent . . . I hope it means the beginning of the end of Leo having to come here.

Clare   I don't think we've quite got to that yet.

Boulton   No? . . . No . . . As you will remember . . . the alternative to you . . . (*He stops.*)

Clare   What about the alternatives?

Boulton   Were not acceptable, family therapy, all that communal exposure . . . no, no. You see Leo on his own, that's fine. I'm sure we're moving towards success.

Clare (*gently*)   In time.

Boulton   I'm watching for changes, I think I can see signs.

He jangles coins in his pocket.

We had a *family* holiday, as you'll have heard. It was amazing, I kept on saying, so this is how it's done! Maybe I was a little preoccupied with my work . . . For the first forty-eight hours. You know my line of work . . . Ready Cooked Meals.

Clare   Ready Cooked Meals?

Boulton   Yes, we devise them for the major chains. I was awaiting news . . . a particular project, a new product.

Clare   What is the new product?

Boulton   A new instant meal, a return to the snack in a cup, you know, adding hot water, but a deluxe version. News of its progress is important to me – in fact I had to stop once or twice to phone as we were motoring along. But there was Leo, on the back seat sometimes singing along to the radio . . . enjoying the scenery. We even had a night of dancing! You know, Brits abroad . . . hair down, doing the conga (*He smiles.*) well, half a conga, the tail of a conga.

Suddenly he gets up.

I'm afraid I need to feed the meter, that's the trouble with these central London locations . . . excuse me . . . I know your time is precious, I'll be right back.

He exits.

Clare *walks over and takes the chewing-gum from where she carefully placed it and puts it back in her mouth.*

Clare (*as Leo*) So – there we are travelling through France. I'm on the back seat and Dad – Dad is going on and on about his work, about whether they're going to OK it – how much he wants it to happen. We're eating all this fucking good food, I don't mind French food, some of my mates mind, but I don't, so we're eating this FANTASTIC food, and Dad doesn't even notice, he's just thinking about his Ready Cooked Meals!

One time we do play a game together, while we're going along . . . Dad's idea of a game, spot the English-made car with a French registration number! Not a great game – a little slow because there's only one every half an hour.

We stay a night in this sort of Holiday Inn, not a proper Holiday Inn.

And Mum insists – she really insists, on DANCING. My dad kind of 'walks' behind her. I'm sitting *watching*, of course. Jesus . . . you should have seen it! She looked so fat . . . gross . . . arms wobbling. No, I'm sorry, that's what she looked like.

Clare *chewing gum for a moment.*

And then in the car the next morning they begin quarrelling about whether they're on the right road. And Mum starts shouting and shrieking, 'I'm map reading – you NEVER believe me about anything, you always think I've got it wrong.' And it's like I'm invisible, on the back seat, like they've completely forgotten there's anybody else in the car. And then Mum, she's shrieking, she reaches down, I promise you and she opens the passenger door while we're going along at sixty miles an hour – she does, only a few inches, but she does. Screaming brakes, emergency stop! Nyeeaaaar, (*Mimics noise.*) yell, yell, yell at each other.

And suddenly it's 'Ssshhh, Leo's there, he's listening' – and then there are these two anxious faces looking at me, my

MUM and DAD, you know blinking at me – like, 'you didn't actually hear anything, did you, Leo?'

Clare *removes the chewing-gum.* **Boulton** *enters. He stands across the stage in a sharp hurried mood, clanking the change in his pocket.*

Boulton   Right, actually . . . change of plan. I think I'd better move, there's a clamping van on the prowl and a traffic warden standing just where I've parked so feeding the meter's not possible. I've two minutes left – still . . . on the meter.

Clare   You're right, parking has become a nightmare in the centre of town.

Boulton   So. We've kept abreast of things, know where we are.

He moves to go.

I have the bank holiday with Leo, now. My wife and I, three whole days to fill, what a prospect! (*Slight nervous laugh.*)

Clare *opens her mouth to speak. He holds up his hand.*

Boulton   No, please, it'll be fine. We'll keep him occupied. No chance to misbehave.

(*At exit.*) Have a good holiday, it's almost the real beginning of summer, isn't it, the first May bank holiday. (*He exits.*)

Gina *enters, a young woman of twenty-two, she is holding an object wrapped up in plastic bags and tied tightly with string.*

Clare   That's all?

Gina   That's all – that was the last appointment – I mean, he was really an extra too, it was meant to be just a ten-minute chat.

Clare   Yes, but I let him, because it was the end of the day. (*She smiles.*) Finally his meter ran out . . . ! But now we're through.

Gina   Except –

Clare   Except what?

Gina   Jess came back.

Clare   She came back? (*Very interested.*) She's not here now?

Gina   No. She came all the way back to give you this.

Gina *puts down the plastic bag.*

Clare   Yes I wondered what that was.

Gina *moves to the exit.*

Gina   Oh, and Mrs Trevel phoned.

Clare   Again? I've already spoken to her *twice* today.

Gina (*at exit*)   She said it was pretty urgent . . . She's going to ring again, should be about now.

She exits.

Clare *is examining with curiosity the plastic bag. She begins to undo the string and take away the layers of plastic, because the parcel is bundled like a surprise package.*

Clare   Jess – a thirteen-year-old girl.

She takes away another layer of the parcel's wrapping.

Jess has been referred to me for over a year. On the NHS. Lives with her mother's new boyfriend in north London. She will hardly attend school at all. Checks in, for half an hour, and then she's off. Instead she moves around the city on her own very particular walks, and things happen to her.

She lights a cigarette.

But she is always on time for me.

She stands near the parcel and becomes Jess, again conveying her essence rather than impersonating a child.

Tell you about an interesting walk, to the video shop. We're in the flat, Fernando, that's my mum's boyfriend, he's as English as me but he likes to be called Fernando. We've been watching some bonking movies, lots of buttocks, a whole afternoon of buttocks. Fernando likes to throw mashed potato at the screen – it's quite good actually, the cold mashed potato sticks to the screen, and the buttocks move up and down through it. Also, there's a movie, somebody's head being bitten off, while he's having sex . . . ugly bastard, it was definitely an improvement without the head!

So I go to the video shop and I choose a movie for him. I know what he likes, by now . . . obviously! And the girl behind the counter she's all pale, and like, when I say, 'Can I have this please?' she ignores me . . . so I ask again, very polite, very nice, and she bursts into tears! And I say, 'What the fuck's the matter?' and she says, 'We're all a bit sensitive at the moment because we were ROBBED yesterday.' Armed robbery, firearms, people being tied up, the whole lot. And then she looks at my video and says, 'Oh no no no you can't have that, it's the wrong certificate, you're too young to see that, it's too violent!' (*She smiles*.) Yeah . . . I thought you'd be interested in that . . .

Martin *enters, a man of forty*.

Martin   I can't believe it – you've finished! (*He smiles*.) Only overrun by thirty minutes.

Clare   Yes. I've almost finished.

Martin (*putting his arms around her*)   Ready for the off – into deepest Norfolk! Beat the traffic, I have a special route of shortcuts worked out (*He grins*.) as you'd expect. And what's more for the whole three days, I have a holiday schedule – hour by hour.

Clare   A schedule? (*She kisses him*.) Oh, I love your schedules – in small doses! I'll give myself over utterly to this one, I think. No responsibility for any plans.

Martin   It's all play and no work, graded in a curve that gets lazier and lazier. I'm not even taking my manuscript, no proofreading. And I bought provisions, including, magically, some samphire. Taking samphire to Norfolk – a more stylish coals to Newcastle!

Clare *returning to Jess's package*.

Clare   Samphire – it's that green stringy stuff, isn't it?

Martin The East Anglian asparagus – we will sit down and guzzle as soon as we get there, hot melted butter dripping all over the place. (*He touches her.*) And you'll be able to leave all the kids behind, all their worries.

Watching what **Clare** *is doing, unwrapping the package.*

And any strange parcels will be left behind as well. What is that?

Clare It's from one of the kids (*She undoes the last part of the wrapping.*) and you won't easily guess what this is. Nor will I. Though I have a general idea.

She reveals what's under all the wrapping. A model, out of cardboard, of the Albert Memorial, covered in its scaffolding. It is a crude but vivid representation.

Martin Jesus – the Albert Memorial! (*He smiles.*) That would have taken some guessing.

Clare She walks around London, this girl – and she started doing these cardboard models, about the things she sees.

She brings them to me – to get a reaction. We have this poker game – she knows I'm going to be boring, clinical, 'why have you made it look like this? What are you trying to show me, Jess?', pushing hard to find what 'statement' she's making. And she's thinking 'why doesn't she just tell me it's fucking good?'

They can be quite unexpected in fact – there's usually something hidden inside.

She lifts the outer part, the scaffolding, off. She then lifts the top of the Memorial off, and then recoils having pricked herself on something.

Shit! what is that?

Martin (*peering into Albert Memorial*) Yes, what is it? I think it's meant to be a giant hypodermic needle.

Clare (*laughs*) That's just like her!

Martin She got hold of a big spike from somewhere.

Clare She gets these ideas – what's growing underneath all those covers on the Albert Memorial?

Martin I should meet her.

Gina *enters.*

Gina I'm afraid . . . I'm sorry, I didn't mean to let her up – I didn't know what to do (*Slight pause.*) but Mrs Trevel is here.

Clare What, right now – here?

Gina Yes. She says it won't take a moment. But it is important. She just wants to ask you one thing.

Clare (*moving*) I know what she wants to ask me.

Martin (*to* **Clare**) Say you've gone already. (*To* **Gina**.) Say she's gone.

Clare No. I don't like to do that. I better see her. (*To* **Gina**.) *For a moment.*

Gina *exits.*

Clare Sorry about this. I've already spoken to her twice today.

Martin (*smiles*) You work too hard – did I ever tell you that? It's a gorgeous day out there . . . and we've got to beat the rush hour.

Clare (*moving the model*) There's something about this time of the year, just before summer starts, when all the parents seem to want to come in and consult. I won't let her stay.

Mrs Trevel *enters as* **Clare** *is saying this. She's in her late thirties, same age as* **Clare**.

Mrs Trevel I'm terribly sorry about this. You can see me, can't you? I know this is wrong, just turning up, I shouldn't be causing an extra appointment . . .

Clare It's fine, Mrs Trevel.

Martin *looks at her, smiles and exits.*

Clare I'm about to leave the office. So this will have to be —

Mrs Trevel (*cutting her off*) I understand. Absolutely.

She sits opposite **Clare**.

This will be the briefest interview. Right. (*Slight pause.*) Deep breath . . . (*Another slight pause.*) I know I've gone on and on about this . . . we've spoken on the phone . . .

Pause. She looks directly at **Clare**.

BUT SHOULD GEORGE GO AWAY? . . . Tomorrow? . . . On his own?

Clare Mrs Trevel, we *have* gone over this, at length.

Mrs Trevel Already. Yes. It's just his first trip away, since all the trouble started, I mean, him curling up in bed, head to the wall, refusing to go to school, and everything.

And now going all the way to Somerset, Upper Slaughter, that ridiculous name for a village, I mean, I know it doesn't seem far, but —

Clare Mrs Trevel . . . we both know I've said this before — I cannot advise you. That is not how I work. Or how this decision should be made. It is between you and your husband, and George —

Mrs Trevel To work it out.

Clare Yes, to work it out. Does George still want to go?

Mrs Trevel Yes, I don't know how passionately, but he does.

Clare So we know that. We know it's tomorrow, and what it might mean to him if it was cancelled, suddenly, after he's been thinking about it for several weeks. And now what is being weighed against that? What are the concerns that count against that, Mrs Trevel?

Mrs Trevel Very judicial. A summing up. Quite right. We're weighing — I'm weighing — against, the fact that this is a very formidable family, he's going to stay with, the Olivier-

Jones's. The father's a very senior civil servant, the boy, the son who's invited George, is incredibly good at everything, and I mean everything, top at French, top at maths, even absurd things like archery. The house they have is huge . . . it all may be intimidating, reminding George how far he is behind.

Pause.

I feel – I just feel . . . (*She pauses.*)

Clare   Yes?

Mrs Trevel   I JUST FEEL . . . (*She pauses.*) the elements, you know, the elements, you know . . . it's delicate. (*She looks up.*) And you spend all this time with George, you know George, you've been looking at what's been going on inside . . .

Clare   Yes, (*Patiently.*) Mrs Trevel, if I may say so, it's not helpful, to think of George as being behind . . .

Mrs Trevel   Yes. You're right. What a fusspot I must appear! I hate to seem a whining mother, and I know my time is up – it is up, isn't it? – but can I ask you one direct question?

Clare   Of course. (*She smiles.*) It'll depend on what it is if you get a direct answer.

Mrs Trevel   Would you tell me – if you thought it was *wrong* for George to go? If you knew it was wrong, would you say?

Clare   Mrs Trevel, I know this seems a predictable answer, a frustrating answer, but it really has to be something George and you talk through.

Mrs Trevel   But if you knew it was wrong?

Clare   If I thought there were obvious factors that –

Mrs Trevel   So you think he should go? Tell me please – I know I said one question, but tell me.

Clare (*trying to remain patient*)   Unless there's anything new that's occurred which I'm unaware of –

Mrs Trevel   On balance? He should go? . . . On balance?

Clare   Yes.

Mrs Trevel   Yes?

Clare   But it –

Mrs Trevel   But it's between me and George. Yes, yes.

Silence.

Clare (*moving at the desk trying to suggest the interview is over*)   So . . .

Mrs Trevel   So – good. Thanks.

But she doesn't move.

There's just one other thing, I know you need to be off. The whole city's about to migrate, isn't it. (*She looks at her watch and laughs.*) There, I've looked at the time for you!
I just wondered, you are going out of town for the holiday weekend, are you?

Slight pause. **Clare** *watching her.*

Clare   Yes.

Mrs Trevel   I have the office number here, and I have your London home number – you were kind enough . . . I don't know if you have two lines there, but I have your number.

She looks at **Clare**.

But is it possible to have your mobile number?

A momentary pause.

Clare   I don't have a mobile.

Mrs Trevel   Really?

Clare   I have no need. I'm usually here, or at home.

Mrs Trevel   Of course. It's just – I'm sure it won't arise, but I would feel – it would be nice – if there was some way of reaching you. If there were problems with George, if I could get in touch.

Clare   I will be checking my number at home regularly. And here.

Mrs Trevel   Of course, if you haven't a mobile, that is the next best thing, obviously. You'll be checking often? Good. (*She looks around.*) I realise all the things you've got to do. I know I'm very fortunate, to be given this time, unscheduled, I'm grateful. I'll leave as quickly as I came in. (*She smiles.*) I can try. Hopefully do no more damage to your weekend. So – I've gone.

She exits. **Clare** *alone on stage.*

Clare   Jesus! (*She moves.*) JESUS! Sometimes . . .

Martin *enters.*

Clare   Sometimes one really wants – (*Lightly.*) to say JUST SHUT UP.

Martin   Absolutely, you should try it.

Clare (*she laughs*)   Oh yeah? And poor George, he's a quiet very watchful child. Big eyes staring at you. Takes his time. Hardly a child in torment. He really wants to go away and stay with his friend.
He's always finding money on the pavement, his speciality. Presents you very carefully with his own pile of coins. (*She moves.*) Certain parents find it very difficult to realise some children just take a pause in their development, to look around, to take the temperature of the next stage. And that's OK.

Martin   I don't know how you stop yourself screaming at mothers like that – (*He mimics.*) Don't you realise it's you that's the fucking problem!

Clare   Yes, well, Mrs Trevel, is the sort, unfortunately, who is horrified at the very suggestion that she should talk to someone. Actually she's usually not quite as persistent as this – (*She moves.*) It was only today . . . it was a little extreme.

She turns abruptly.

She wanted the number of my mobile, you know.

Martin   Oh, Christ! You didn't give it to her, did you?

Clare   No. (*She moves.*) I'm only away three days – and she wants the mobile!

Martin   What a nightmare that would be – her popping up while we're having a bath . . . or at three in the morning.

Clare   But she'll still be calling the home number, she was already getting in the mood for it. 'Is it all right for George to go to bed so late?' A whole barrage, expecting a quick response.

Martin   Leave the machine off. So she can't leave a message.

Clare   No, that wouldn't be a good idea.

Martin   Why not? All your possible urgent cases, the real ones, have the mobile number, don't they?

Clare   Yes. (*She moves.*) I'll think about it . . .
She'll just call here anyway, (*Smiles.*) swamp the machine here.

Martin   But it's perfectly possible to say you don't constantly check the office number at the weekend – because you don't.

Clare (*lightly*)   I don't know, it's getting very complicated, Martin.

Martin   No, it isn't. (*Lightly.*) It's making sure you're not a slave to modern communications. And more important, it's establishing a zone – free of Mrs Trevel!

Blackout.

Scene Two

Clare *walks on, lights a cigarette.*

Clare   Jess – on the news.

She becomes Jess.

I don't know why they don't have *music* while they read the news on TV. It really sounds EMPTY because they don't have music – ALL THE WAY THROUGH. Not yet. I'm going to write and suggest it – because they'd get a lot more people watching.

You know the weathermen, when they do the weather they change the weather, the maps, by stepping on a pedal on the floor, they do, I read about it!

So I've had this idea, the news, while they're doing it, they can sit with these pedals under their desk and when there's a really sad item, some people dying in a war, they can play the sad pedal – and when there's something a bit better, they can give us the trumpet pedal . . . you know, they can work it like an organ! Their little feet tapping away! NEWS WITH MUSIC!

She moves.

The other thing about the news is, everybody that comes on, absolutely every time, they always say, 'But, at the end of the day . . .' doesn't matter if it's about politics or fish fingers, out it comes – 'But, *at the end of the day* –' like everything makes sense now. Wow! But, at the end of the fucking day, they have, in fact, not said a fucking thing!

Clare *sits, starts chewing gum.*

And Leo, on the news.

She becomes Leo.

The news on television is real – a lot of the time. But sometimes when there isn't enough, they make it up.

They have a special room, where there's this one man, only one, who *thinks it up*. So when they don't have enough, they

send for him, and he says, 'What sort of thing do you want?'
And they tell him. And then he invents it.

He does! And he gets paid really well. Only works three days
a week. Good job, that!

She exits.

Empty stage, we hear the tape-machine, **Mrs Trevel**'s *voice loud,
coming over main auditorium speakers.*

Mrs Trevel   Could you call me . . . this is Caroline Trevel,
George's mother, as soon as you get this message, please.
There's no answer from your home phone number. Please.

Gina *enters, morning light, she stands by answering machine, rewinds
the tape a little, and then stands very still listening to it.*

The second message comes out of answering machine on stage: **Mrs
Trevel**'s *voice, very urgent.*

Mrs Trevel   I'm now here . . . on a train . . . please ring
the following number . . . that's where I'm heading as soon
as you get this message, there's still no answer from your
home.

The message clicks off. Then there's a really loud, imploring voice.

RING ME. PLEASE. RING ME.

Gina *stands for a moment staring down at the tape machine.* **Clare**
enters. **Gina** *startled.*

Clare   You're here very early, Gina.

Gina   Yes. I woke at five thirty this morning, for some
reason. And I had a few things to do in town – so here I am.

Clare   I usually beat you to it – (*She laughs.*) I'll have to
start getting in earlier! Did you have a good weekend?
Manage to wind down? Do anything exciting?

Gina   It was fine. It was very satisfactory.

Clare   Very satisfactory! (*Laughs.*) You're always so
cryptic, Gina – come on – that could cover a thousand sins!

Gina (*coolly*)   I did a couple of tasks I've been putting off doing. It was OK. Things worked out.

Clare *realises she is not going to get any more.*

Gina   I was listening to the messages – they're all from Mrs Trevel.

Clare   Yes, well, I was rather expecting that. I had a weekend largely free from calls. I somehow managed it. It's usually pretty difficult for me to have a real break. I keep wondering about various cases –

Gina   But not Mrs Trevel.

Clare   No.

Gina (*crisply*)   I'll make some coffee. (*As she exits.*) I think there are eight calls on there in all.

Clare   Eight!

She presses the machine.

Mrs Trevel   You *must* ring me – it is absolutely essential you ring me.

Gina *enters.* **Clare** *doesn't look up, she is suddenly preoccupied.*

Clare   On any of these calls – does she say if anything's happened?

Gina   Mrs Trevel is here.

Clare (*startled*)   She's here? Now?

Gina   Yes. She's just come in. She says she'd like to talk to you. (*Slight pause.*) If she could.

Clare (*impatient with* **Gina**'*s contained manner*)   Well, show her in . . . !

She pauses for a moment, straightening herself.

Mrs Trevel *enters.*

Mrs Trevel   There you are . . .

She stops.

First of all, to get one thing clear, you *are* agreeing to see me?

Clare Of course. Of course I'm agreeing. I hope everything's well . . . with George, and –

Mrs Trevel Why didn't you return any of my calls?

Clare I just got your messages now. I was literally listening to them, this very moment, I only got back this morning –

Mrs Trevel I tried, goodness knows how many times – I left messages here, again and again. And there was no answer – never any answer from your home number.

Clare I've explained, I've only just got in –

Mrs Trevel Didn't you check your messages here – for heaven's sake? Didn't you hear me asking for you?

Momentary pause.

Clare Has something happened, Mrs Trevel? Has something happened to George?

Mrs Trevel I will be coming to that.
I just couldn't believe, after the discussion we had, just before the weekend. I could not *believe* I got no reply –

Clare What has happened to George?

Mrs Trevel Didn't you see the news? On the television? What were you doing all the time – didn't you see a single bulletin?

Clare No. I didn't happen to watch any television.

Mrs Trevel Or the radio, you didn't catch the radio – you were too busy for THAT EVEN.

Clare *trying to remain calm.*

Clare Mrs Trevel, just tell me what's taken place? Where is George?

Silence.

Mrs Trevel's *head bends for a moment.*

Clare Are you all right?

Mrs Trevel   HE RAN AWAY.

Clare   What? Where to? He's been found, hasn't he?

Mrs Trevel   It was on the *news* bulletins – child of eleven *missing*. Seeing it on the national news, George's picture . . . they asked for a photograph, George's face staring back out of the television – you can't imagine the shock, seeing that.

Clare   Mrs Trevel, has he been *found*?

Mrs Trevel   There were helicopters, police dogs, police radios buzzing all the time. AFTER TWO DAYS, AFTER NEARLY TWO DAYS, THEY FOUND HIM . . . You can't believe how long that seemed . . . that's when I so wanted you, to be able to speak.

Clare   It must have been incredibly worrying. Please just tell me – if you can, what happened? Where did they find him . . . ? (*Quiet.*) Where is he now?

Mrs Trevel (*suddenly*)   Of course he's *alive*. Otherwise I wouldn't be here. He's safe now.

Clare   Thank God for that. (*Quiet.*) I'd assumed he was 'all right', but . . . what a terrible thing to have to go through. (*Momentary pause.*) Do you think you could tell me the sequence of events, when you're ready, how it happened?

Slight pause.

Mrs Trevel   I don't know how you missed the news. I really don't. It wasn't on every bulletin – but even so, how on earth did you miss it?

Clare   With respect, I don't think that's what's important now . . . It would really help me to hear the complete facts, as soon as that's possible – and of course I must see George. Where was he found?

Slight pause.

Mrs Trevel   At the bottom of the garden.

Clare (*startled*)   What do you mean?

Mrs Trevel   There's a clump of trees, a wood, at the
Olivier-Jones's, a rather horrible wood at the bottom of the
garden. He was there, he'd built this sort of hide – out of logs
and dead branches, and other things . . . He was there, at the
bottom of the garden.

Clare   Oh, I see – . . . so it was like he decided, possibly as a
dare, to spend a night in the woods . . . It was like camping –

Mrs Trevel   It wasn't camping. It was NOT camping.
Are you suggesting we didn't look hard enough?

Clare   No, of course not. Any child that doesn't want to be
found for two days – that evades the police and all that –
obviously something is going on there that we must –

Mrs Trevel (*cutting her off*)   You think he just went off for
an adventure . . . in the woods and *I* blew it all up into
something enormous. Is that what you think?

Clare   *No*. Again, of course not. I was just making the
point, rather unnecessarily, that he didn't 'Run Away', in
the sense of running off to the city, or hitching along the
motorway. This is something different . . .

Mrs Trevel   I can't *believe* you said that . . . That he went
camping.

Clare   Please, let's not get stuck on this. It really is not
what matters. When can I see George? The sooner the better,
obviously.

Mrs Trevel   You won't be seeing George again.

Slight pause.

Clare (*startled*)   Really? You mean he won't be coming to
any more sessions?

Mrs Trevel   What else could I have meant? It's best to be
blunt, isn't it?

Clare   I understand you being upset, of course, and angry
about what's occurred. It's natural –

Mrs Trevel   You needn't worry about George. He's just
not coming here any more.

Very slight pause.

Clare   If that continues to be the situation, Mrs Trevel,
then I can give you the name of a colleague, because it's very
important somebody talks to George.

Mrs Trevel   You really don't need to concern yourself
with any of that. George is nothing to do with you now.

Clare   No. Mrs Trevel.
I do have to insist that I have contact with whoever is going
to see George, so I can liaise with them –

Mrs Trevel (*suddenly*)   *Why* was there no answer from your
home number? – From your home answer machine? Why did
it just ring and ring?

Clare   I realise it must have been very maddening, not to
be able to contact me. But I have to say it is very unlikely I
would have been able to do any more than the police – who
were on the spot.

Mrs Trevel   Yes. Naturally you would say that, wouldn't
you. *So* – did I miss your explanation? Or didn't you give me
one?

Momentary pause.

Clare   I will answer all your questions, about phones, if
you like, in due course – but I think we've *got* to get George's
arrangements clear.

Mrs Trevel   Was the answering machine faulty, or had it
been left off?

Clare (*very slight pause*)   I believe it was left off – I was in a
great rush getting away, as you may remember.

Mrs Trevel *takes out notebook, and starts writing.*

Mrs Trevel   I'm just making a note of that. You don't
mind, if I make a note? (*As she writes.*) And of course, no

checks were made on your machine here. At the office.
Where all my messages were waiting for you?

Clare It *was* a holiday, I was trying to have a genuine
break. Now . . .

Mrs Trevel A 'genuine break' . . . (*She notes this down.*) Of
course.

She closes notebook.

I'm running out of time for this interview. I have things to
do. I was here on a reconnaissance –

Clare A reconnaissance?

Mrs Trevel Yes, I think that's the right word. I wanted to
hear your explanation.

She holds notebook tightly.

Which I now possess. You must forgive me if I've been rude
. . . Maybe I haven't been rude. (*She looks at* **Clare**.) You
don't have children, do you?

Clare No . . .

Mrs Trevel *gets up.*

Mrs Trevel I have no idea, at this precise moment, where
this reconnaissance is going to lead. Whether there's going to
be a second stage – or not. I just know you're not going to see
George again.

Clare I would urge you –

Mrs Trevel FORGET GEORGE.

She moves.

What should interest you far more, is whether you'll see *me*
again . . .
Or whether you'll be totally free of me.

She moves off.

I expect we've cleared things up . . .
I just have to consider the position . . . What do you think?

She exits.

Clare *alone for a second. She is startled by the encounter, but begins to recover her cool.* **Gina** *enters with coffee.*

Clare   You're a bit late with the coffee, Gina. (*She smiles.*) Might have helped break the atmosphere a bit, if you'd come in while *she* was still here.

Gina   I'm sorry. I couldn't find the tin.

Clare   Mrs Trevel was quite upset, understandably. I will need to dictate a long letter to her *today*.

She looks searchingly at **Gina**.

Did you see anything on the television, about George, did you catch any of it?

Gina   No, I didn't see it.

Clare (*sharp*)   But you *know* what I'm talking about – you know what happened to George?

Gina   Yes. I do now. I *just* saw a little story, on the inside page of the newspaper . . . right this very moment, only a few lines, with 'Boy Found' . . . and George's name.

Clare   Yes. (*Smiles, relieved.*) I *thought*, if you'd known Gina, you would have warned me . . . before she arrived.

Pause.

Gina (*walking up to her*)   There's a list of your appointments for today. And there's somebody waiting to see you.

Clare   Who?

Gina   It's a surprise. *He* wants it to be a surprise. He says you'll know him.

Clare   OK. A very *brief* surprise, please, Gina.

Gina *exits.*

Clare   In fact I'm not exactly in the mood for surprises this morning.

Richard *enters. He is nineteen years old – a beautiful tall boy.*

Clare *doesn't recognise him.*

Clare   Hello? Yes?

Gina   This is –

Richard   No. Don't say my name! Please!

He stares across at **Clare**.

Hello, Miss Attwood.

Clare   I'm sorry. You'll have to help me. We know each other, right?
But at the moment – I can't quite picture . . .

Richard   I'll give you a clue – five and a half years ago . . . I sat here, opposite you.

Richard *grins*.

Clare   Well, I guessed *that*. But (*She's staring at him.*) I'm still not quite –

Richard (*charming smile*)   And – I was wearing, the last time I was here with you, I was wearing a shirt with huge mock ink stains all over it . . . Remember? Pretend blotches.

Clare   Richard! Of course. Richard Mellinger! Jesus, for a moment I just couldn't . . . you're so tall now! Such a big lad!

Richard   I grew a little. Yes. (*He grins.*) So people say. Five years is nothing for you – but for me . . . !

Clare   Where have you been, what you been up to?

Richard   It's been great, I've been in America. On a foundation course.

To **Gina** *who has been watching with interest.*

Can I just have a moment? Alone with Miss Attwood?

Gina *exits*. **Richard** *turns back to* **Clare**.

Richard   I promise it'll *only* be a moment.

Clare   You look really well. I can't believe it's you . . . tanned . . . relaxed . . .

Richard Yes. (*He grins.*) I could feel you scanning me.
(*Teasing.*) Feel that gaze panning across me – got to about
here now, haven't you? (*He laughs, indicating his elbow.*)
Noticing things, picking up clues . . . ?

Clare No!

Richard (*grins*) Oh yes. Beaming in on anything, my wrist
watch, or whether I'm looking you straight in the eyes!

Clare (*laughs*) I'm not on duty, yet.

Richard I want to tell you all about it. About me. Not
now, I realise!
I brought this for you . . .

He gives **Clare** *a present.*

It's just the smallest thing, not a serious gift.

Clare *opens it, it's a large elaborate black necklace.*

Clare How exotic, Richard. (*Warm smile.*) It's great,
lovely.

Richard Thought you could wear it when you were
dancing, you know swing it around, as you bop.

Clare (*laughs*) And clear the floor, probably! Decapitate a
few people . . .

Richard I know I mustn't take up time, I want to make an
appointment so I can see you properly.
I expect a drink is out of the question – me taking you out for
a drink?

Clare An appointment would be better.

Richard Right. I'll keep everything for then, because now
you've got the whole day ahead of you – full of spotty kids,
rabbiting on about Mum and Dad, how they hate the
dentist, how they're being beaten up at school – they're
probably even worse than I was.

Clare (*smiles*) And look at you now! Yes, I'd love to hear
everything, Richard.

Richard Right. Good.

Clare (*warmly*)   I'm still working out . . . if I *was* staring it's because I'm still looking for where that little boy is, in that face, the little boy that used to sulk in the corner.

Richard (*charming smile*)   Well, look hard. It *is* me.

Clare   I like your clothes, Richard. That's a wonderful jacket – and –

Richard   And Italian shoes – that's right!

Clare   Very cosmopolitan.

Richard   Yeah, that's the word! (*He grins.*) I'm working hard at it anyway, to be cosmopolitan. I think it's a great thing to be.

He moves.

And I've been away so much . . . just walking around town these last few days, London has CHANGED.
I mean, I'm amazed at the difference, whole clusters of buildings have shot up – looking like they don't belong here at all.

He moves up to her.

I'm off. I just wanted to surprise you –

Clare   And you did.

Richard   When I see you properly – I'll tell you things, to make you laugh. My exploits, adventures, *and* my qualifications. Hope to impress you.

Clare (*gently*)   You don't need to impress me, Richard.

Richard   I'm going to leave it like that . . . tantalising . . . OK?

Richard *kisses her on the cheek, and leaves.*

Gina *enters.*

Gina   Who was *that*? He was gorgeous!

Clare   Wasn't he just . . . (*She smiles.*)
I never heard you so enthusiastic about anything, Gina.

Gina *watching her.*

Clare   Sometimes they sprout like that, transform . . .
become confident. And it's great to see.

Blackout.

Scene Two – A

Clare *enters wheeling a large flat trolley, on it a large flat object
covered in plastic.*

Clare   Jess, after her success with the Albert Memorial –
managing to surprise me, not to mention drawing blood
(*Looks at her hand.*) – was definitely a success in her eyes.
So – she's announced she's now embarked on her own *series* of
models – the landmarks of London.

She lights cigarette, and moves trolley forward.

(*As Jess.*) OK – first up, I've done Harrods for you.

She surveys the big bundle on the trolley.

Before you look at it, and knowing how keen you are in seeing
'statements' in whatever I show you, I think a word of
explanation is in order.

And the explanation is – to take you on a bit of a walk. You
know how good I am on walks!

This is a shoplifting walk . . . right here, in the room. Yeah –
I thought that would get a reaction out of you.

The thing about nicking things in those stores – and it is so
obvious I don't know why many people don't do it – the
answer to the problem is, to EAT THE EVIDENCE. Yeah –
eat it all.
To go around nicking food and eat it before you leave the
fucking place. What they going to do – pump out your
stomach?
Here it is.

*She reveals large vivid cardboard model of Harrods, covered in
Japanese flags.*

So you're going through the Food Hall, OK, are you with
me? Marble everywhere you look – and the tourists are there,
shuffle, shuffle, very slow – and the people who *live* round
there are pushing through very fast, 'Excuse me, can I get by,
EXCUSE ME.'
What they really mean – is – 'Out of the way you fucking
foreign gits, wish you weren't in our city – but we need you
. . . so – excuse me.'

And in the middle of all that, I'm taking a king prawn here, a
chocolate truffle there – it's great, you should try it – and
above all CRYSTALLISED FRUIT, the easiest thing to
nick in the world, because of the handy round boxes.
And I'm shovelling them down me as fast as I can get hold of
them. Tastes disgusting after a bit of course.

So – you got that?

Now, look, (*Indicates model.*) Harrods, very recognisable I
think you will agree.
The Japanese flags are there, because I think that will be the
worst thing any of *them* could imagine – if the JAPANESE
bought Harrods. *And* –

She takes the Harrods dome off the model.

The top comes away and coming out of it is –

Out of the dome sticks a large plastic object covered in gunge.

This is meant be part of a giant sneaker. A SNEAKER – yes –
is that me? Does that 'represent' me? I don't know, you tell
me.

And it is coated – as you can see and this is the good bit – with
CRYSTALLISED FRUIT. These are the actual things!
The whole dome – oozing crystallised fruit, like there's so
much in there, it's just got to *get out*!

What d'you think? That's Harrods! I hope when you next see
the real thing, it'll look exactly like that to you. – Yeah.

I want to make you look at all of London different – before
I've finished with you.

Scene Three

*Large model, in Jess's distinctive style is carried on upstage. It is much
the largest one yet.*

*It is a section of the white Nash terraces that overlook Regent's Park –
the roof/cupola raised on the central house – and out of its top is
sprouting a mass of spiky, futuristic aerials and satellite dishes, like a
great tangle of wire hair.*

*Music, as if from a bandstand, is drifting across the park, there's also a
picturesque environmentally conscious rubbish bin in the shape of a
wooden squirrel.*

Clare *is lying in the middle of the stage, on her front, sunbathing. She
is scantily clad, barefoot, the straps of her dress partially pulled down,
so she's lying barebacked. She's talking on her mobile phone, as she lies
on her front.*

Clare   *Come on*, I'm famished.

Where are you? At the top of Baker Street! Well, HURRY
UP. There's a band playing here and everything, it's perfect
picnic weather . . . and you're still lumbering up Baker
Street!

You know where I am? . . . What d'you mean between the
Nash terraces and the water? – That could almost mean any
part of the park! . . . Yes . . . near THAT tree . . .

No, I'm not . . . I'm stretched out – I was in a real erotic
reverie – and I'm going back to it . . .
(*She laughs.*) Who says it was about you! . . . I *thought* that
might make you walk faster! . . .

*She rings off, puts mobile phone away in her bag and lies down flat on
her stomach.*

For a second **Clare** *is alone with the music.*

Mrs Trevel *enters. She is wearing dark clothes. She is very bundled up for such a hot day. For a moment she leans against the rubbish bin, watching* **Clare**.

Clare *turns her head truly startled. For a moment she is at an incredible disadvantage. She sits up pulling up the straps of her dress trying to maintain her dignity.*

Clare   Mrs Trevel . . . !

Mrs Trevel   I thought it was you.

Clare   Heavens – what a surprise!

Mrs Trevel   It is – isn't it.

Clare   I was just taking my lunch hour . . . I very rarely do this . . . especially *here*. I work so close to the park – and yet I hardly ever use it, but today because it was so *hot* . . . (*Glancing at* **Mrs Trevel**.) It seemed a good idea.

Mrs Trevel   You really don't have to explain yourself to me. You're lying in the park, in your lunch hour – what could possibly be wrong with that?

Leaning against the litter bin, she takes out a cigarette.

I'm sure the park is full of other professionals, right at this moment – head teachers sunning themselves . . . topless hospital administrators . . . civil servants in bathing trunks, . . . maybe even a partially nude senior policewoman . . . Letting all the stress go. (*She smokes.*) Why not?

Clare (*lightly*)   Slightest sign of the sun and the British go mad, don't they nowadays. We rush out, tearing off all our clothes.

Pause. They look at each other. **Mrs Trevel** *glances at all the clothes she's wearing.*

Mrs Trevel   All except me, it appears. (*She blows smoke, smiles, relaxed.*) I'm sure the wheels are going round now . . . 'Why is she bundled up . . . is it because of some deep fundamental problem? . . . A complex about her body?'

Clare   Please, I didn't mean –

Mrs Trevel (*breezily*)   No, of course not.

She laughs.

I'd really confuse things now, wouldn't I, if I took my shoes off . . . started losing layers . . . !

She smokes.

Don't worry about it, no offence taken. I startled you after all.

And I know you're wondering two things.

Did I see your mobile phone?

And – am I here by complete accident? A bizarre coincidence.

Slight pause. She smiles.

Or am I in fact stalking you?

Clare   Stalking me! (*Startled laugh.*) That's very American. I thought that normally happened to famous film actresses, why would you want to do that?

Mrs Trevel   So you believe in coincidences then?

Clare   It depends, obviously, on the circumstances. In regard to this one – right now – I haven't made up my mind.

Mrs Trevel   Yes, well, it would be a rather surprising turn of events, if I was following you all over London, I agree. (*Pause, she laughs.*) I mean, that would be a wonderfully strange thing to happen.

*The mobile phone rings faintly from inside **Clare**'s bag. **Clare** glances up at **Mrs Trevel**.*

Mrs Trevel   Answer it, please, answer it.

Clare (*already taking phone out of bag. Into phone*)   Where are you? . . . Only there! . . . you're making very stately progress . . . (*Quiet, confidential.*) It would be a good idea, to hurry up. If you can.

She puts the phone away calmly.

It belongs to my partner – the phone. Recently acquired. He was phoning from a few streets away. He's just about to enter the park – I hope, with the *food*.

Mrs Trevel   You're having a picnic together? Matching lunch-hours, that's very well co-ordinated.

Clare   So how is *George*?

Mrs Trevel   He is absolutely fine.

Clare   And do we know any more about what happened?

Mrs Trevel   It all took place when you were away, on holiday. Don't worry about it.

Clare   And forgive me pursuing this point, have you arranged for him to see somebody else? I left several messages for you, you didn't call me back.

Slight pause.

Mrs Trevel   I think I'm going to really shock you, Miss Attwood. But I'm not interested in why George ran away.

Clare (*startled*)   I can't believe that.

Mrs Trevel   Yes, isn't that incredible. It does shock you, doesn't it. I can see.
But what interests me – what fascinates me, at this precise moment – is *you*. Is what happened between us. For some reason, I can't get that out of my mind.
Why do you think that is?

Slight pause.

Clare   Well, almost certainly because you've been through a very traumatic experience. Losing a child, not knowing where that child is – that is, obviously something very major . . .

Mrs Trevel *lights another cigarette.*

Mrs Trevel   Go on. (*She looks at* **Clare**.) Tell me more.

Very slight pause.

Clare   The first time I went to New York, at the age of
eighteen, I was walking along by Central Park, I suddenly
heard these yells, this terrible shouting. It was coming from a
very tall man – and in front of him was this tiny girl, of about
five. His daughter, he had evidently just that moment found
her, after she'd wandered into the park alone.

And his whole body was shaking, and this huge man was
literally screaming 'Never, never do that again', with such
ferocity – I mean *really* terrifying. It was like he was
completely possessed by rage and relief.
It's always been an indelible picture, a visual example for me
of –

Mrs Trevel   Of the kind of thing I went through? And you
think I've sort of got stuck in this rage and relief? It's an
interesting idea . . . and I am taking it out on you?

Clare   No, that is not what I said.

Mrs Trevel   Like somehow I've got stuck, in third gear?

Pause. Pleasantly, softly.

You really think you're going to get away with just that?

Martin *enters with picnic. A large elegant hi-tech picnic basket.*

Clare   There you are . . . (*She turns.*) This is Martin
Pender.

Mrs Trevel   The partner – we brushed past each other,
didn't we, on that important day –

Martin   Hi. (*He is warmly polite.*) Nice to meet you.

He puts down the picnic basket, pointed smile at **Clare**.

I didn't realise you had company.

Turns back to **Mrs Trevel**, *who is looking closely at picnic basket.*
He watches this, pauses for a moment.

Are you joining us? . . . Please join us.

Clare *has been trying to signal him not to do this.*

Mrs Trevel Join the picnic? . . . You're too kind. (*She laughs*.) Maybe you should consult between yourselves. No, I won't barge in further.

Clare *relaxes for a second*.

Mrs Trevel I'll just have one piece of fruit. If I may. A peach.

As **Martin** *hands her the fruit*.

I *love* that – a post-modernist picnic basket.

Martin It's good, isn't it. (*He smiles*.) People covet it like mad.

Mrs Trevel I'm sure. And a great spot for a picnic too . . . (*She gazes around*.) those white terraces . . .

Clare Amazing aren't they – in the sun. I often wonder what goes on in them.

Mrs Trevel (*to* **Martin**) So what do you do?

Martin I'm an academic. Of a kind. A transport consultant.

Mrs Trevel So to go with the sunbathing policemen and the head teachers . . . we have a transport consultant.

Martin (*puzzled by this*) Quite. (*Then he smiles*.) I'm shortly to have a book published in fact. The result of several years labour – (*He laughs*.) too many years in fact!

Mrs Trevel What is the book about?

Martin *hesitates*.

Martin People usually miss a beat, when I tell them. The book is on – the Metrobus. The *London Metrobus*.

Mrs Trevel (*without missing a beat*) Of course. Why not? (*She smiles*.) What is the London Metrobus?

Martin It's the driver-only operated bus that has now taken over ninety-seven per cent of London routes. The sort you sit behind in your car, cursing, because you can't get by, waiting for all those people to lumber aboard and pay their fare.

Mrs Trevel   Yes, I know that feeling, absolutely.

Martin   Good. I was hoping you'd say that!

He is laying out the picnic, beginning to demonstrate his thesis with pieces of food.

To be strictly accurate there are two sorts of Metrobus, the Metrobus proper, and the LEYLAND TITAN, wonderful name isn't it, redolent of the seventies . . . I nearly used it as a title.

The thesis of the book is – it's the first major calculation ever of how many billions of pounds London has paid in congestion, in lost business hours, for taking a simple and idiotic decision to abolish the bus conductor!

Mrs Trevel   Yes! Everybody in this city can follow that argument.

Martin   Good. Yes! (*Encouraged by her interest.*) If this a Metrobus (*With sandwich box.*) because of the extraordinary narrowness of the thoroughfares, the major arteries, in this town, and the fact that we don't have a set bus fare unlike almost every other Western capital, the whole of London is congealing. *The book shows the way forward.* (*He smiles.*) Now, the average Metrobus –

Clare   Martin – Mrs Trevel can wait for the book to come out I'm sure.

Martin   Sorry. (*He grins.*) I can never resist a captive audience. (*Turns to* **Mrs Trevel**.) And what is your work?

Mrs Trevel   'My work'? (*She smiles.*) I don't do any at the moment – but I was once an Index Compiler. Or a Member of the Society of Indexers – to make it sound a little grander.

Martin   Really? (*Lightly.*) You could have done my book then . . . !

Mrs Trevel   Maybe. (*She blows smoke.*) If I was still practising . . . (*She looks at both of them.*)

When I've finished this peach, which I almost have – I will be gone.
It is idyllic, with the band playing.

Pause. She bends her head studying the ground.

Of course if you look on the ground . . . then you begin to see things, see what's happening in our parks, hypodermic needles, the inevitable used condoms, even some false teeth . . . it's gradually spreading . . . (*She smiles.*)

I even saw a rather muddy vibrator in the middle of the flower walk in Kensington Gardens, the other day.

She breaks off, moves slightly, glancing at the ground.

Sorry, I must stop peering around, I thought I saw something, (*She looks up.*) but it's obviously just –

Martin (*smiles*)   A form of displacement activity?

Mrs Trevel   I'm sure that's the right term. Yes.

Clare   Martin uses even more jargon than I do.

Slight pause.

Mrs Trevel   Delayed gratification . . .

Martin (*taken aback*)   Excuse me?

Mrs Trevel   Delayed gratification . . . that is one of my favourite pieces of jargon from your world, Miss Attwood, children having difficulty with . . . 'delayed gratification'.

Clare   When all we mean is they can't bloody wait for anything!

Mrs Trevel   That's right. Sometimes, occasionally, just for fun, I invent jargon. (*She smokes.*) 'Traumatic Overhang' . . . that kind of thing . . . 'Slow Lane Reversals' . . . children passing close to 'Dangerous' Information.

Clare   Well, 'Dangerous' Information is genuine jargon (*She smiles.*) I've even been known to use it. It's over emotive I agree.

Mrs Trevel   Yes. Well . . . (*She throws her finished peach stone into the litter bin.*) I've finished. Better begin to pick my way over all the basking flesh –
(*She smiles.*) I'll probably get arrested for having *too much* covered up!

She begins to move off.

Martin's *mobile phone begins to ring.* **Mrs Trevel** *stops and stares towards the ringing mobile in* **Martin**'s *pocket.*

Martin   It's all right, the bastards can wait. It's on the answer machine.

Pause.

Mrs Trevel   So, you've got one too.

Clare   Yes he has.

Mrs Trevel   For some reason, I don't know how I got the idea . . . just now I thought he was ringing from a call box, and you had *his phone*.

Clare (*calm, defiant*)   No.

Pause.

Mrs Trevel   It is an extraordinary time for professional people like you, isn't it?

I mean, in the old days, when you were out of the office, you were generally out of reach.
But there's the mobile culture now – and that vulnerable moment when you've just finished a call . . . and just about to make another, and it rings and *people can get through*.

She smokes.

So who gets the Mobile Number? Maybe nobody at all. But, perhaps you're the sort of person that *likes* to be available to certain *cases*, part of the service.

So then it becomes one measure – an important measure – of who gets put on the 'A' list.

Tough decisions have to be made. And then what lies, sometimes a whole spiral of little lies are necessary, aren't they, to keep particularly neurotic fuss-pots at bay. Like over protective middle-class mothers, who are demanding access which they patently don't deserve.

Clare   Mrs Trevel, what do you want? Tell me what I can do for you, now.

Mrs Trevel   These are clearly delicate problems – difficult to get right.

But if it goes wrong, you make a mistake – then it can only be temporarily embarrassing, awkward, but no more. One would have to be extremely unluckly, to get some sort of nutty avenging angel, coming at you all over town. Suddenly popping up everywhere, in the park, behind you on the escalators in the tube, or even in the bar, in the interval at the theatre.

Pause. Slight smile.

Yes, that would be unlucky, I agree.

She exits. Silence.

Martin   Jesus . . . !

Clare   Yes. Quite. (*She moves.*) FUCK, SHIT, FUCK, SHIT, FUCK FUCK! . . . Just thought I'd get that out!

Martin (*grins*)   I love it when you're analytical.

Clare   Well, I don't like being caught unawares! And what's more, *thanks* for inviting her to stay at the picnic.

Martin   What could I do? She was looking at the food! It was either that – or telling her to shove off. (*Smiles.*) Which might have been risky . . . !

Clare   Yes. But you were interested too, weren't you, in having a good peer at her.

Martin   I've heard a lot about this woman, it's natural to want to take a closer look.

Clare   Well, we certainly got one! (*Self-mocking smile.*) *And* she happens to appear when I'm stretched out half-naked! I could say this was all your fault . . .

Martin No you couldn't!

Clare No . . .

Pacing.

OK, you want a quick burst of analysis? Well, I DON'T
KNOW . . . I don't know what she's hoping to achieve. It
can't just be because she didn't get the attention she feels she
deserves. The phone calls and all that. Of course I feel guilty
about what happened – does she want that demonstrated
further? (*Sharp smile.*) Although it's far from clear what *did*
happen. She doesn't seem remotely concerned with the
reasons behind George's actions . . .

Maybe she exaggerated the whole disappearance – and he
was so embarrassed by his mother's behaviour – he wouldn't
come out of the woods! (*She moves.*) Maybe something is
going on in the marriage . . . if I could get to the husband
now – he seems a well-adjusted sort of character. Or even
better, if I could get *her* to see someone, a colleague.

Martin No chance. There's no chance of that, *whatsoever*.

Clare No. (*She moves.*) It'll burn itself out. A few more days
– and she'll begin to cool down.

Martin You love it anyway. You love the challenge of it.
Whatever it is she's up to.

Clare (*mock rage*) Don't you *dare* start on that – that's
rubbish.

Martin (*smiles*) Right . . . OK . . . fine . . . (*Slight pause.*)
But you do . . .

Clare No . . . (*She moves.*) And certainly not in this case.

Martin *watches her, smiles.*

Clare Well, come on – we've only got a few minutes more
of this picnic, it's all she's left us.

She smiles. Starts eating.

I couldn't help thinking of George, and the way he's always
finding money on the pavement. And there SHE is,

surveying the ground in all these parks, and finding RUDE LITTER! It must be in the genes.

She touches **Martin**, *warm, teasing*.

Come on then – are you going to give me some calm, dispassionate advice?

Martin   Advice! . . . *You* want advice?

Clare   Why not?

Martin (*grins*)   Right . . . (*Slight pause.*) Run like hell in the opposite direction!

Clare (*warm laugh*)   OK . . . Great.

Martin   So are you going to advise me about the Book Launch?

Clare   Book '*launch*' . . . I didn't realise it was going to be that showbizzy!

Martin   A volume on the Metrobus – what do you think? (*He laughs.*) One can but dream! No – I don't mind if nobody reads it. I don't. (*Slight pause.*) It's really solid, like its subject. (*Serious.*) It's the *work, that counts.* (*Forceful.*) *It is.*

Clare *warm, touching him*.

Clare   Absolutely! That's right.

Blackout.

Scene Three – A

Clare *standing in long coat*.

Clare   Jess – on FAME.

(*As Jess.*)   It's not worth it. Take it from me – it's just not worth it.

I came round the corner the other day in Soho – it was just off Wardour Street.
There were a whole lot of photographers, crowded together

like flies – round this model or actress. And suddenly she spins round and she's holding up her hands, like this!

She does it palms outwards.

And they're covered in blood! Yeah – fake blood – I'm sure – but blood! And she starts screaming at them . . . freaking them, their mouths wide open, and she's holding up her bloody hands right in their faces! (*She does it again.*)

I don't know who she was – but she's gone completely crackers, already!

She sits.

And GEORGE, on FAME.

(*As George.*)   My English master, Mr Brownjohn, gets really cross about this radio programme *Desert Island Discs* – do you know it? Where famous people get asked to choose music they'd like to play at sea.

He comes in on Monday mornings and says I can't BELIEVE who was on *Desert Island Discs* yesterday. They haven't done nearly enough to deserve to be on! He says. It's an absolute disgrace, why on earth did they invite that person, he's NOTHING! My teacher gets so *angry* – he says he's going to write and complain because it makes a nonesense of the whole thing.

Pause.

Do you think Mr Brownjohn will ever get on it?

Scene Four

Clare's *office.* **Gina** *brushing her hair, ready to go out.* **Richard** *sitting watching her.*

Gina   She won't be long.

Richard   Good. (*Slight pause.*) I can wait. I'm very used to waiting here.

He looks across at **Gina**, *as she puts her make-up on. Her very contained manner.*

You're very different to Mrs Haggerty.

Gina   I'm sure I am.

Richard   She was here in my time, she seemed very old then. I expect she was only fifty.
All the kids would sulk while they waited, I know *I* did, and the parents looking a bit ashamed . . . thinking 'OH my God I hope nobody walks in who knows me!' The English are by far the worst about this, aren't they – about having their children 'seen to' –

Gina   (*brisk*)   That's not true any more – it's getting much better.

Richard   Right! . . . (*Glancing around.*) And Mrs Haggerty sat over there, and she just chatted all the time, really cheery, never stopped.

Gina   I don't tend to chatter.

Richard   No. (*He grins.*) I think I'd worked that out.

He gets up, moves over to her.

Where are you going tonight?

Slight pause.

Gina   Out with friends.

Richard   Out with friends . . . Ah! (*He smiles.*) That sounds promising.

Close to her. Flirting with her.

Maybe you completely change – after a certain hour. Suddenly this exotic, incredibly daring person appears . . . this creature of the night! (*Teasing smile.*) Is that what happens?

Gina   That's not quite how I'd describe it. (*Slight pause.*) But I know how to enjoy myself.

Richard   That's great . . . I know how to do that too! I
think I'm pretty good at it by now. (*Watching her contained
manner.*) So how *do* you enjoy yourself? . . . Lots of drugs? . . .
Frenzied karaoke? . . . Or maybe sitting at the computer
sending masses of seductive e-mail all over the world?

Pause.

Gina   I have been known to do two of those three.

Richard (*very curious*)   Really . . . ?

Gina   Yes. (*She looks straight at him.*) And *one* of them rather
often.

She moves across the room.

Richard   I went to a Rave for the first time, the other
night. They're already out of date apparently, maybe this
was the last one! . . . It was behind the gasworks in King's
Cross. People were dancing in weird ways.

He imitates.

Looked very strange to me . . . and sometimes they did a
little flourish, with their hands – that reminded me of my
parents dancing, when I was tiny. It was very unsexy – but
what do I know? . . . I've only been in America. (*He grins.*)
Nothing happens there!

Clare *enters in smart evening-dress, she is wearing earrings.*

Clare   There you are, Richard.

Richard   You haven't forgotten?

Clare   Of course not.

Richard   You look amazing. What's it for? Where are you
going?

Clare   Oh, it's just a fund-raising function, rather formal,
it's for a children's charity.

Richard   Everybody's heading somewhere? Why not? It's
a great summer's evening out there.

Clare (*turning*)   So, Gina – you can go now. Have a good time.

Gina   Thanks. I think I will. If it all goes according to plan.

Gina *exits*.

Richard (*laughs*)   'Goes to plan' – she's a funny girl isn't she!

Clare   She's very good at her job. She's just extremely self-contained.

Richard   You look really great in that dress!

Clare   Thank you.

Richard   You should have looked like that during our sessions!

Slight pause. **Clare** *smiles*.

Clare   So, Richard . . .

Richard   Where to begin?

Clare   I don't know. (*Lightly*.) Where are you going to begin?

Richard   I want to fill you in about America – it was great! I did well, I think, on the course.

Clare   Naturally. You were always a very bright boy.

Richard   I brought some pictures. Where are they? (*Shuffling in his pockets*.) I know other people's pictures are the most boring things in the world. So for you, it's selected highlights! A few of my friends, several cross-country journeys, a couple of landmark moments. (*He smiles*.) It was an interesting time. . . . I want to do it justice.

About to show photos, **Gina** *enters*.

Clare   Yes, Gina.

Gina   I've got bad news. Well, it may be bad news – Mrs Trevel is here.

Clare   *NO*. She can't do this now. Not again. I have an appointment. Tell her, I have an appointment.

Gina   I was literally just going out, and as the door opened – she was there.

Clare   *I will not see her*.

Gina   I couldn't stop her – she pushed past. She must have been waiting for the moment.

Mrs Trevel *enters carrying a very large box-briefcase, and two other bags*.

Mrs Trevel   Yes – I pushed past. But it's OK I can wait, I'll wait outside. (*Indicating* **Richard**.) You can deal with him first, if you like.

Clare   I cannot see you now, Mrs Trevel, it is out of the question. We can discuss making an appointment, for some time later – but I am simply not able –

Mrs Trevel (*calmly*)   Oh yes you are.

Richard   Yes, yes. You do *her*.

Clare   Richard, *you're* the one with an appointment.

Richard *is taking in* **Mrs Trevel**'*s appearance with all her bags*.

Richard   No, no please. I'd rather not have somebody waiting to come in. Pacing around outside. The conditions have to be right to do this. I'll go for a walk. No, I will, and come back and see how you're doing.

Clare   Ten minutes, Richard!

Richard   Oh yeah . . . less. (*As he exits*.) You have a good time now.

Mrs Trevel   What a handsome boy! One of your old clients? Come back to see you? Must be good when that happens, pleasing, when they *want* to see you.

Clare *watching* **Mrs Trevel** *closely*.

Clare   Yes it is.

Gina   Would you like me to stay, Miss Attwood?

Very slight pause.

Clare   No, Gina, that's not necessary. You go off for your evening.

Gina *looks across at* **Mrs Trevel**.

Gina   Actually I've just remembered I've got a phone call to make, so I'll be out there for a short while.

Gina *hesitates and then leaves*.

Mrs Trevel (*smiles*)   She's going to wait . . . she's worried about you. (*Moves.*) Of course, you can always get her to drag me out of here.

Clare (*unfazed*)   Let's hope she doesn't have to do that.

Mrs Trevel *moves purposefully into the middle of the stage, sits and opens the large briefcase with a very loud click. It is stuffed with papers and files, which she begins to spread in stacks, around her chair.*

Mrs Trevel (*as she does this*)   You look splendid, dressed like that. A successful busy woman, and you still manage to look elegant, unhurried.

Clare   I'm going out later, to a function. My partner is picking me up.

Mrs Trevel   Your partner . . . (*She smiles.*) He's always turning up on time, isn't he? You obviously have a deeply convenient relationship.

Clare *watching her*.

Clare (*sharp*)   We happen to have an engagement tonight, that is why this is not a good time –

Mrs Trevel *suddenly looks up.*

Mrs Trevel   Look, I think we crossed over a boundary, didn't we, in the park. At least *I* feel we did. And now it's time – to use that awful expression – for the gloves to come off.

Clare   So you feel you're in a fight, do you, Mrs Trevel?

The briefcase and files being organised, crisp noises.

Mrs Trevel   Just need to get this ready . . . I know you're wondering how big a pickle you're in.

Clare (*calmly*)   Am I in a pickle?

Mrs Trevel   Any moment –

Clare   Mrs Trevel, if you want to complain about me, if you think I've done my job badly, there's a structure to deal with that, there is an ethics committee –

Mrs Trevel *looks up innocently.*

Mrs Trevel   This isn't about whether you're good at your job, Miss Attwood. Whether you were giving the right treatment . . . It's more interesting . . .
I think you're probably a fair to good practitioner, middle of the road, not too stupidly dogmatic about following just *one* approach, either being a Kleinian or whatever the other one was called . . . isn't that so?

Clare   I *try* not to be over doctrinaire.

Mrs Trevel   Good. (*She is poised, ready.*) So, you asked me in the park, *what I* wanted.
And I have thought of one thing I want from you. For all the children you deal with – you compile files, don't you? I'm sure they're considered highly secret. I want the files that you keep on George.

Slight pause.

Clare   You know I can't give you those Mrs Trevel.

Mrs Trevel *looks across at her.*

Mrs Trevel (*calmly*)   I think you will give them to me, by the time I finish.

The papers spread around her.

I've got something here which I want to use, to show you.

Because I realise I must seem like the Mother from Hell to you – I hate that expression too – but it probably accurately sums up what you think of me. And I thought you were

·entitled, to a couple of illustrations of why I was behaving like I am . . . OK.

Clare *watching her.*

Clare   And what have you got there?

Mrs Trevel   This is what *I* consider – 'dangerous information'.

Clare   Dangerous information! About what? About me?

Mrs Trevel   No no. (*She laughs.*) Is there some? No, no, it's not about you, Miss Attwood . . . !
'Dangerous information' means, doesn't it, information that could be difficult or confusing for that child to cope with?

She moves papers around.

This is dangerous information that George sees.

She holds up newspapers.

Firstly, this is a well-known *broadsheet* newspaper. On the day, the very day, a child serial killer is found guilty and it is all over the front page, a truly *terrible* story. On the back page of the *same* newspaper there's the cheerful headline, a trailer for a feature, 'HAD ENOUGH OF SERIAL KILLER CHIC . . . ?'

She looks up from the paper.

Isn't that extraordinary?

Clare   Yes . . . I can't really respond, Mrs Trevel, until I know where you're heading.

Mrs Trevel (*watching her*)   Doesn't it show you how everything is sliding together, news and entertainment, one great big wash of ephemeral rubbish.
My husband, who is an accountant, not a literary man, but he likes to coin expressions – he's not particularly good at it, but he does it. (*Waves newspaper.*) And he calls this phenomenon '*Gleaze*' . . . sleaze and glitter. Everywhere, things are merging.

Some papers flutters off her across stage.

Oh dear, there goes another piece of dangerous information.
Let's leave it there for a moment, ticking away.
Come to this one – Market Testing.

She holds up a form.

This is a market-testing questionnaire from when George
and I visited our local toy museum. It is asking the question
'Is the museum correctly oriented' – strange phrasing I agree
– 'towards the right market – Is it properly targeted?'
As we walked away together, George said,
'Mummy, am *I* correctly oriented towards the right market?'

Clare   I don't believe he said that, I think that story's
fiction.

Mrs Trevel   *He definitely said it.* It made me realise we'll
soon be market researching our children immediately
they're in the womb, identifying the niche for them to aim
for, and seeing which genes need a bolstering.

Clare   Mrs Trevel, I have parents all the time obsessed
about giving their children the right start. Talking about
moving house immediately to live next door to the best
school, or even creating false addresses to make sure their
child gets in. I have them agonising about the *food* they're
giving their children, a *whole* fake industry is growing up of
potions and special foods to make your child into a new
improved human being –

Mrs Trevel (*slight smile*)   You're responding now? You
think you know where I'm heading?

Clare   – And I tell all these parents, in a variety of ways but
I tell them, there is time. There IS time. Slow down. And
they do.

Watching **Mrs Trevel** *with papers.*

And so should you.

Silence. **Mrs Trevel** *is immersed in the big briefcase, seemingly
oblivious. Papers fluttering everywhere.*

Mrs Trevel   I'm looking for something very small. (*A paper shoots across stage.*) Whoops, there goes another! We'll leave that there for a moment.

She rummages.

Small and *yellow* . . .
I think it's in this bag. (*Plunging into her handbag.*) There are little leftovers here from our holiday in America, (*Lightly.*) a few dollars, this mace . . . (*Produces can.*) you know the spray for blinding muggers . . . Is it illegal, by the way to carry that in this country?

Momentary pause.

Clare   Yes. It is. I should get rid of it if I was you.

Mrs Trevel   Yes, well, I wouldn't need this on a summer night in London, surely! (*Pleasant laugh.*) Don't look like that . . . your assistant is standing guard outside after all! (*Blithely.*) Then again, maybe a little frisson between us is good.

Very slight pause, she puts the mace down in front of her on the table. She then produces a tiny yellow newspaper cutting.

So here it is.

Clare   *That's* what you were looking for?

Mrs Trevel (*holding it tight*)   So this is the Future – I cut it out and kept it as soon as I read it.

She is about to read it then stops.

You know what worries me most, how confident everybody is when they pontificate about the New Technology. About how paradise is just round the corner, especially for children – able to 'communicate'.

Clare   It *is* second nature for most kids now, the new technology.

Mrs Trevel   Really? That's what they all say. Even the actual words, Internet, Superwhatnot, Cyberspace, sound frightfully smug, don't they, pleased with themselves?

She smoothes out the yellow cutting.

The only thing we can be *certain* about is – people are
ALWAYS wrong about the future.

Clare   But *you* were just telling me how people would treat
their pregnancies in the future.

Mrs Trevel (*smiles*)   Naturally I am the exception. (*She
indicates cutting.*) This is how the future seemed in 1971 and
they were so sure . . .

'By nineteen ninety-eight, MASS AIR TRAVEL WILL BE
A THING OF THE PAST' . . . !

She looks up incredulous.

– 'the cost of criss-crossing the globe will have become
prohibitively expensive because of energy costs . . . This will
lead to the REBIRTH of indigenous cultures – and a
consequent decrease in violence.' Amazing, isn't it!

Clare   You must be one of the very few people that keeps
predictions –

Mrs Trevel (*continuing to quote*)   'Young children will be
able to walk the streets with ease, without any fear for their
safety.'

She throws cutting back into her bag.

In other words, a return to the safe world of my childhood
. . . when it was so much, undoubtedly so very much –

Clare   No. *No.*

Mrs Trevel   What do you mean, no?

Clare   I mean, no, that is wrong. This is the Golden Age of
Childhood argument, the recent past was so much better.
I'm afraid if there's one thing I'm sick of hearing it's that
myth being peddled. I really am. Every other parent I see
comes out with it.

Mrs Trevel   But it *was* so much easier and *safer* when I was
a child –

Clare   Since I know you don't like jargon, Mrs Trevel –
that is bullshit, utter crap.

Mrs Trevel (*startled quiet*)   I can't believe you think that.

Clare *moving over to drawer*.

Clare   I want you to hear something. Children had very
real fear then. Worse maybe . . . listen to this.
I want you to listen to this child.

Mrs Trevel   So you *tape* all the children as well . . . whose
child is this?

Clare *produces old tape-recorder from drawer with tape already on it.*

Clare (*switching it on*)   An old tape-recorder . . . for an old
tape.

A soft young **Girl's voice** *starts, with a slight Lancashire accent.
The* **Girl's voice** *is half a whisper, very private in tone. There is the
sound of music, a pop song from the early sixties, behind her voice and
the sound of a family around on the stairs. The effect is intensely
evocative, laughter from somebody outside the door, voices of a family
half heard.*

Girl's voice (*secretive*)   In one moment I'll do it, Dad is just
on the stairs – just got to wait for him to go down. So there's
no chance of anybody coming in . . .

Mrs Trevel   What a lovely voice . . . who is this child?

Slight pause.

Clare   The only child I can play without asking anyone –
it's me . . . at the age of ten and a half.

Mrs Trevel   It doesn't sound like you at all.

Clare   My family had just come down from the North,
from Stockport. The year before. You can hear my accent
just beginning to go . . .

A man's voice butts in to the room for a moment, the girl answers.

Mrs Trevel   And that's your father?

Clare   Yes. (*She listens to her father calling.*) There he is . . .

Mrs Trevel A nice warm voice.

Clare *stops the tape for a moment.*

Clare I kept an audio diary, I used to play music with it, snatches of my favourite records, and then things from the radio, compile little items of my own. (*Slight laugh.*) The days before the video diary . . . I tried to make sense of the world on tape.

She plays tape.

Now listen, please.

Girls voice I'm afraid . . . I can't get it out of my head. I'm very afraid they're going to let off the BOMB, really soon. Blow up everything, scorch my school, the end of all the buildings I know, melt the playground. *SSShhh* . . . hang on a moment.

Sixties music from tape.

Mrs Trevel This is very strange, it really is . . . listening to this with you. Eavesdropping – on you as a girl.

Girls voice (*continues*) We drove past a golf course yesterday, Mum and Dad, and Sarah and me. These men strutting about – I imagined them all being fried, as they played golf, caught by the flash, burnt to a cinder like toast. But still standing up, standing absolutely still like sentries, all these burnt golfers – and the whole course completely, really really black. As far as I could see . . . (*Her voice hushed.*) It was *frightening*.

Clare *stops the tape.*

Mrs Trevel No, don't do that, please – don't stop it. (*The tape restarts.*) The music, it's so good . . . hearing that music. It's probably playing on the same sort of cheap red gramophone I had.

Clare I usually stop here. It's just some singing now . . . me humming to my records.

Mrs Trevel No, please leave it just for a second – . . . doesn't it really get to you? It gives me goose-pimples . . .

being transported back into the past like that. (*As the singing continues*.) We must be roughly the same age, (*She smiles*.) though tonight you look much younger than me of course. But it is the *same* music, I listened to.

Clare I'm just aware of my rather off-key 'singing', if you can call it that. The previous part of the tape is what's interesting –

Mrs Trevel I know I know. But listen . . .

She is moving, very intrigued, the music stops for a second.

Other sounds from outside the girl's room, fill the tape and the auditorium.
She suddenly turns.

My God – did you hear that? And again . . . ! *That*?

Clare What?

Mrs Trevel That hiss . . . there. That sort of spitting hiss . . . ! Don't you hear it?

Clare (*startled*) A hiss?

Mrs Trevel It's a TROLLEYBUS! It is, that sound there. I promise you! An extinct trolleybus – it's passing right under your window.

The noise brushing close.

Oh my God, that does make me almost shake . . . I haven't heard that sound, not since, since I was a girl.

For a moment the sound moves all around us, and then begins to recede.

Clare Yes, well, it was probably the last trolleybus running through Acton . . . its final journey!

Mrs Trevel You can almost smell the leather, can't you? See the young girls chattering together, and those big tickets you got given, for the old dark pennies. And all those fat stubby cars of your youth . . .

The music comes back.

You stopped to change a record, as a girl, and *there* was that sound, in the gap, coming out of that street at us. And so *clear* . . .

Hear the ringing too . . . ? Very faint, there! That belongs to one of those sleepy old police cars – charging somewhere.

Pause. The sounds slip away.

That was great . . . !

As the music resumes playing.

I feel an overpowering urge sometimes – I just want to go back to that time so much! I'm terrible about the past . . . (*As the girl sings.*) Want to climb back into it . . . When everything was easy, the future was bright, there was a job round every corner if you wanted it . . .

She turns.

Wouldn't you want to go back to that time? Even briefly?

Clare   No. Absolutely not.

She walks towards the tape, as her young self sings out. The singing getting louder.

I was in a tiny room, right next to the loo. I had a lot of nightmares in that little bed. And outside that window – the world seemed rather dangerous.
As I think I've tried to show you.

She stops the tape.

And now you really must allow me to continue with what I was doing. Richard is coming back at any moment.

Mrs Trevel   Yes, where is he? –

Clare   And Martin is picking me up soon –

Mrs Trevel   But for the moment we're alone. I expect your assistant's left by now. (*Calmly.*) Now, are you going to give me the files I want? On George.

Clare   No, of course not. I thought I made that clear. But there's really nothing that important in those files, you should put them out of your mind. (*Slight pause.*)

Mrs Trevel (*calmly*)   I know you think I'm a rather old-fashioned sort of person, you do, don't you, an under-employed mother who has nothing better to fill her days than constantly fussing about her children. But you're wrong. That is not the case.

Please give me the files.

Clare   No. It would set a precedent that could have all sorts of implications.

Facing her.

Mrs Trevel, you can try the law if you like. You can try litigation – no doubt we're going the American way and there will be litigation about absolutely everything. Just as over there, nobody apparently is responsible for any of their actions – if you murder your parents it must be because they abused you, even if you can't remember them doing it. Or because your favourite game show was suddenly rescheduled!
And if your child runs away, it must be because the therapist wasn't at the end of the phone! But finally we have to look *inside*, not at all these external matters, but look at ourselves.

Mrs Trevel   So you're not going to give me anything? . . . I see.

Clare   So – now if you could . . .

Mrs Trevel   You think you've handled this pretty well, don't you? Risen to the challenge?

Suddenly she swings round.

You LIED to me. (*Coming at* **Clare**.) *And what's worse, you just lied to me again!*

Clare (*very startled*)   What? I *haven't* just lied to you –

Mrs Trevel   Yes you have. What *is* the point. WHAT IS THE POINT IF YOU DO THIS! TELL ME? YOU KEEP LYING TO ME.

Suddenly she hits **Clare**, *glancing blows.* **Clare** *turning away as she comes for her.* **Clare** *manages to catch hold of her arms, powerfully restraining her.*

Clare   Mrs Trevel, just calm down (*Really strong.*) YOU'RE GOING TO CALM DOWN NOW.

Mrs Trevel's *eruption subsides. She breaks away.*

Mrs Trevel   Yes, yes . . . (*Slight smile.*) very sound advice. (*Pause, she laughs.*) I must be stuck in that third gear, mustn't I. (*She moves.*) She's absolutely BARKING, that's what you're thinking . . . (*Slight pause.*) I'm sorry.

Pause. She faces her.

You're such a clever woman, Miss Attwood, I mean a genuinely impressive person. Maybe a little arrogant, but imaginative, and not really that aloof, unlike a lot of people in your position.

Why is it, that I feel so strongly I've got to finish you – finish your career? To put it at its crudest – to do my best to reduce you to nothing.

Pause.

Clare (*startled, quiet*)   I had no idea that is what you were trying to do, Mrs Trevel. (*Slight pause.*) But it will seem different in a few days, it will be less intense.

Mrs Trevel   You think things will change in the morning? Maybe you're right . . . (*She moves. Pause. She smiles.*) I admit what I'm trying to do is pretty difficult.

Martin *enters. He is wearing a fashionable suit.*

Mrs Trevel   He arrives. Not on a white horse, but he arrives. As you said he would.

Martin (*surprised*)   Hello . . . Mrs Trevel.

Mrs Trevel *straightening her hair, her head bent.*

Martin Are you all right?

Mrs Trevel Yes . . . (*She moves, pause, smokes.*) What a display . . . ! (*Pause.*) It'll sound a bit ridiculous if I say, have a good evening . . . but have a good evening.

She exits. Silence.

Clare (*quiet*) That is one rather disturbed lady . . .

Martin You mean she's fucking crazy, that's what you mean!

Clare If you like . . . she just went for me, just before you arrived, semi-attacked me.

Martin Really? Are you OK? (*Coming up to her.*) What did she do?

Clare I'm fine . . . (*She smiles.*) . . . I think! No, it's all right . . . When she tries to bludgeon her way to what she wants it's easy to deal with.
(*Pacing.*) I'm definitely going to involve some colleagues. Make sure George is all right, bombard her with letters, *try* to get her to see someone.

Martin Yes!

Pause.

Clare It's as if I've become every professional to her – every lawyer she's had to deal with, every teacher, every doctor . . . It's like she wants to bag one, take out a professional. (*Warm smile at* **Martin**.) Talking of which – you look good.

Martin Yes. (*Grins.*) I like it too. I thought I'd wear this for the great presentation. Don't look so blank! You know at the Queen Elizabeth Conference Centre – World-wide transport conference. *My lecture.* I'm beginning to think it's time for me to develop a rather more svelte look.

Clare (*warm smile*) You should . . . (*She moves.*) Richard never came back. You didn't see him? I wonder what happened . . .

She is moving towards tape machine. Quiet.

She can't get me, can she?

Martin Get you? You mean do you harm professionally?
Mrs Trevel! Of course not.

Clare No, I don't see how she could . . . there's no legal
way . . .

Thinking about it softly.

I don't see what she can do . . . (*She smiles.*) Anyway, I'm up
to it. (*Self mocking laugh.*) After all she even promoted me,
during the session, from a 'fair to good practitioner' to a
'genuinely impressive person'!

She switches on tape, her younger self softly hummming to pop tune.

Martin (*studying an A–Z closely*) It's such a great night out
there, I thought we could walk to this 'do'. I've been working
out a way to get to Lincoln's Inn Fields, taking in a couple of
interesting places on the way, a couple of really obscure
crannies, one of which I've never even heard of . . . ! It has
the most wonderful name, Long Lost Yard . . . I've planned
an elaborate –

He looks up.

Who's this? What's this tape?

Clare *standing by tape.*

Clare Oh, it's just from a few years back.

Pause.

It's only a girl singing.

Her young self continues to hum along to the record.

Fade.

Act Two

Scene One

Hot strong sunlight.

Clare *is standing by her desk, three Plasticine figures like misshapen dolls standing in a row on the desk. Two of them are dressed in clothes, bits of old denim etc., one of them is still wrapped up in dirty newspaper, completely covered.* **Clare** *faces us.*

Clare   I came in a few days ago – and these squat little figures were waiting for me . . . wrapped up in newspaper, standing in a line on my desk.
They are in fact rather sturdily made, out of grubby Play-doh. Later that day Jess turned up, for an appointment. Bang on time as always.

She begins to unwrap third Plasticine figure.

(*As Jess.*) I see you've only unwrapped two of them – what are you trying to tell me? . . . they're no good?

By the way, what did you think of Marble Arch? – Best one yet, wasn't it?
Did I tell you, when I dropped it off, I met your partner, I really hate using that fucking word – I expect *you* do too . . . But you probably *have* to use it, don't you! Anyway, I met your 'partner', your boyfriend, your bloke – he's just right for you, isn't he – a bit shaggy, really calm and soothing, but quite funny . . . in a laid-back way. And he was really interested in my models. Yes!

Third figure coming out of newspaper.

And when I've told you about *these* – you'll want them on your mantelpiece, at home. You will!

Moving, holding the figure.

You see, I thought, let's look at this place – like the tourists do. See the city as they see it.

So first – we've got to call the policemen 'Bobbies'
(*Pronouncing it with ludicrous American/Cockney accent.*) – the only
people to use the word BOBBIES are Americans – like they
say 'Where are your cute London BOBBIES . . . ?' (*She
smiles.*) And you don't know what the fuck they're talking
about . . .

And the second thing – YOU HAVE TO GO TO
MADAME TUSSAUDS. Oh Yes . . . ! You know, the wax
museum.

Because every time you pass there, it doesn't matter what
day of the year it is – there's a truly FUCKING
ENORMOUS QUEUE. Have you noticed that? – There is
ALWAYS a queue. *All tourists.*

And for that reason – nobody that actually *lives* in London has
been inside that wax museum for years and years and
years . . . ! Anything could be going on in there, couldn't it!?

So – *I* went inside. I did. Just sneaked round the front of the
queue, it was dead easy.

And you know what I saw . . . ? It was a very hot day . . .
And all these models, the wax models, they were beginning
to MELT.

The Prime Minister had shrunk a bit, one ear had run down
the side of his chin . . . Prince Charles's face was sort of
sinking into his chest, so the top was just one big misshapen
ball, and the American President – he was going at the waist,
and one of his legs was melting smaller, and curling round, so
it was like a little tail.

No point you looking like that – you haven't been in the
BLOODY PLACE have you? . . . since you were ten
probably! So you have no idea what's happening there . . . so
shut up!

And I thought – stuff all these Politicians and 'Pop
Performers' . . . ! They should have a room, about my age
group, about the FUTURE.
Yeah. You know the 'Football fan of the future' with his

machine gun held next to his football scarf, that sort of thing, and the 'Schoolkid of the future', with her porno virtual reality goggles for when she's playing in the playground.

So there we are – (*She lines up the three figures.*) that's who they are. The funny thing is – you're ever so cool when I show you these things, you think that'll stop me bringing them to you . . . make us talk deeply instead – about my *insides*. But it just makes me bring them all the more.

Clare *exits. The light changes, soft sunlight.*

Martin, **Gina**, *bustling around.* **Martin** *quite animated and nervous.*

Clare *enters – breezy, relaxed, moving over to her desk.*

Martin   So, Clare – here's your ticket. Put it somewhere really obvious, safe, *now*. Are you clear which entrance you should go to?

Clare   Absolutely, (*She smiles.*) don't worry.

Gina   It's your big day, Mr Pender.

Martin (*grins, trying to hide his nerves*)   My 'big day', Gina, yes. (*He looks at her.*) Pity you can't be there too . . .

Gina (*flatly*)   That is a pity, Mr Pender. Yeah.

Martin (*laughs*)   You'll be able to watch the highlights, when they bring out the video.

He moves.

The most important lecture of my life – and it is scheduled for the Friday afternoon before the August bank holiday!

Clare   Everybody will stay for it. Don't worry. (*Warm smile.*) How could they not . . .

Martin   All *two thousand* delegates? Maybe! Even the representatives from Macedonia . . . ? (*He laughs.*) All going to get the full benefit of my encyclopaedic knowledge of the London Metrobus . . . !

Gina   Will they be interested? In the Metrobus? – I mean the people from Macedonia?

Clare (*smiles*) Of course they will. Anyway, it's a great launching pad for your book.

Martin Yes. And at least nobody will be able to shout back – I absolutely disagree! What a load of bollocks, you've got it all wrong! For this afternoon at least I will be the acknowledged world expert, on the Leyland Titan! (*He smiles.*) And how we went wrong organising the city's transport.

He turns to **Clare**.

Did I mention you need to be there about twenty minutes before I'm on? Better make that half an hour. And I'm on at *15.15* – which is –

Clare I know. I know! Yes. I'll be there. (*Warm smile.*) Don't *worry*.

Martin (*producing booklet*) Yes . . . I'm on just after the Canadians and their talk – 'Mono-rails, Dead or Alive?' (*He moves.*) I'm going off to rehearse now, in a quiet back passage at the conference centre. I've just been going over 'The Insiders guide to the REALLY BIG Public Address'. (*Laughs.*) It's made me even more nervous! Don't use all your best jokes right at the beginning, it's that kind of thing. And introduce a *pause* exactly ONE THIRD of the way in, a sort of stumbling incompetent pause, like you've completely forgotten what happens next – makes them all sit up in an instant apparently. (*Smiles.*) Electrifies the bastards.

Clare (*going up to him*) It'll be OK, it really will.

Gina Best of luck, Mr Pender.

Martin Yes. (*He kisses* **Clare**.) Well, you'll probably find you're sitting directly in my eyeline . . . maybe that'll be a good thing! I'll do it all for you . . . it'll give it a personal feel.

Clare Right. (*Warm laugh.*) And I'll be mouthing back, it's going great.

Martin (*grins*) I'm going to give them something to remember! (*He exits.*)

Clare Right. (*She moves back to her papers, to herself.*) Put my ticket exactly where I can find it. Good.

Gina Shall I move these . . . ? (*She hesitates by the 'dolls', disapprovingly.*) These figures – ?

Clare Yes. If you could. (*Sharp.*) Not *those* ones!

Gina *is moving two brown boxes that are also on the desk.*

Clare Those are some personal things from my father's. From his old office.

Gina (*putting them back*) Sorry. I didn't realise.

Clare Yes – I don't know why it's taken eight months after his death, for them to let me have them. But there we are. I picked them up this morning from the solicitor – *he kept me waiting*, naturally. I parked in the underground car park, in Marble Arch. Can you remember that? –

Gina Yes, Miss Attwood.

Clare Because I was running late – I left the car there. It will have been there all day. You will remind me, Gina, that's where it is?

Gina Yes. I will.

Clare Great. (*Her mood breezy, relaxed.*) So, I've just got a short talk with Mr Boulton – what does he want I wonder? – and then Richard's rearranged appointment, and then you're *free*, Gina.

Gina Yes.

Clare Another chance to get out of town. What are you doing *this* holiday weekend? Going somewhere, got something special laid on?

Gina Oh, this and that. Watering the window box . . . getting in some Chinese food – (*Slight pause.*) and maybe something else.

Clare (*warm laugh*) That sounds nice and mysterious! Tell me. Just for a change, tell me, Gina.

Slight pause. **Gina** *hesitates.*

(*Warm smile.*) Or tell me half? How about that? (*Trying to be friendly.*) Is that a deal?

Very slight pause.

Gina   I'd rather not. If you don't mind. (*She moves.*) If it's all the same to you. (*Slight pause.*) Excuse me, I thought I heard the bell . . .

Gina *exits.* **Clare** *smiles. She opens one of her father's boxes, peers in, takes out a dusty old sixties office toy. Silver balls that knock together. She gives them an amused look.*

Gina *enters.*

Gina   Mr Boulton is here.

Boulton *enters, carrying a large bag. A beat behind him,* **Mrs Trevel** *enters. She is dressed in summer clothes, she seems far more relaxed, dark glasses, her hair different, much more attractively dressed.* **Gina** *watches for second, then exits.*

Clare (*to* **Boulton**)   Hello . . . (*Then she sees* **Mrs Trevel**.) Mrs Trevel! What are you doing here? This is *Mr Boulton's* appointment.

Mrs Trevel   I know. (*Breezily.*) That's all right.

Boulton   If you don't mind – I would very much like Mrs Trevel to be here.

Clare *looks from one to another.*

Clare   For what purpose?

Mrs Trevel (*sitting demurely in corner*)   I'd be very interested if I could sit in, if I may . . . ?

Boulton   Yes –

Clare   I'm afraid all appointments with me are completely confidential –

Boulton   But this is not a private matter. It doesn't concern *Leo.* This is more social . . . it'd just help me if Mrs Trevel was here.

Mrs Trevel (*low laugh*)   Bet that surprises you!

Boulton   *Please*.

Slight pause.

Clare   Well, only if it has nothing to do with Leo, and if that's the case I'm not really sure why we're meeting . . .

Boulton   Thank you. She can stay? That's very good of you.

Clare   But if there's *anything* that does touch on Leo (*To* **Mrs Trevel**.) – I will have to ask you to leave, immediately.

Boulton   Of course. We understand.

Clare   And I haven't a lot of time. My partner is giving a lecture later today, which I have to attend, and I have various things to do before then . . .

Pause. **Boulton** *looks at her*.

Boulton   So . . . Now . . .

He hesitates.

What I want to do will surprise you, I think. May seem a trifle odd, initially (*He smiles*.) you may even think I've taken leave of my senses.

Clare (*trying to keep the atmosphere relaxed, laughs*)   This is some build up, Mr Boulton – what could you possibly have in mind?

Boulton   Yes, well – (*He laughs*.) it's not what typically happens in here! It'll seem like excessive behaviour . . . (*Smiles*.) But in fact it's not. All I ask, you bear with me, for just a few moments, because it will *become* crystal clear, in a minute, what I'm trying to demonstrate.

Clare   Of course . . .

Boulton   And this is one of the reasons for Mrs Trevel being here, to help me with the tasting.

Clare (*startled*)   The tasting?

Mrs Trevel (*laughs*)   The tasting . . . sounds promising, doesn't it!

Boulton *reaches into his bag and takes out a package. Inside, done up with string, is a fistful of Cadbury Flakes.*

Clare (*smiling*)   Chocolate . . .

Boulton   Yes, the Chocolate Flake – one of the great pieces of confectionery, I think we'll agree, ever created. An icon even, in the world of cheap chocolate. And its date? When do you think it dates from . . . ? Yes, go on, guess! (*Unable to wait.*) I'll tell you, 1920!

Clare   Really? I had no idea. That's much earlier than I would have guessed.

Boulton   Yes, I know, 1920! Of course the Flake has more recently become identified with its erotic advertising, but in fact it has *already* lasted over three quarters of a century.

Mrs Trevel (*smoking*)   Remarkable, isn't it!

Boulton   And here – (*Produces another package.*) the legendary Kit Kat, and it dates . . . ? (*Slight pause.*) from 1935! Yes the days of Hitler, and the airships, and the great ocean liners.

Mrs Trevel   I really love Kit Kat, I used to stuff myself with them while I was revising for my exams –

Boulton (*to* **Clare**)   You can have some, please, go on.

Clare (*smiles, nibbles a piece*)   Thank you. I'm not often offered sweets by parents, I can tell you!

Boulton   No? There's something almost perfect about the Kit Kat isn't there. To be controversial, it's almost Mozartian! Yes . . . And then of course there's Maltesers from 1936 . . . the ones with the less fattening centres. All these have lasted longer than most books of the period, most plays – I must *stress* this isn't about nostalgia, but I'm asking, as I expect you've guessed, is it possible to create classic confectionery, *now*, in present circumstances? Something that will endure?

Clare   So this is what really concerns you at your work? Is that what you're telling me?

Boulton   Just wait . . . wait one moment.

He produces out of his large bag, a collection of fresh vegetables.

I'll do this very quickly, I promise . . . I'd just like the chance
to show you, (*He smiles.*) don't get alarmed . . .

He is arranging the vegetables in front of her.

Mrs Trevel (*lightly, to* **Clare**)   You're going through a
phase of people *bringing* you things, aren't you! Firstly it's me
and my old newspapers, now it's vegetables.

Boulton   Yes. So − (*Having arranged vegetables.*) In our
efforts to relaunch the Meal in the Cup . . . to transform it.
And I don't think one could have a less fashionable product
to relaunch, could one? . . . The very bottom end of the
market, of Ready Cooked Meals . . .

Mrs Trevel   That is certainly true.

Boulton   So here's the array of vegetables that went into
our first mix, the prototype. Potatoes of course, tomatoes, all
the obvious, *plus* broccoli, *three* sorts of mushrooms, several
kinds of onions, courgette, aubergine and a really
imaginative idea − some JERUSALEM ARTICHOKES.
Though I say it myself, an inspired touch . . .

Mrs Trevel (*helpfully*)   They were trying to recreate a
strong farmhouse taste.

Boulton   That's right. (*To* **Clare**.)   I don't mind you
smiling −

Clare   No, I wasn't. I wasn't smiling.

Boulton (*smiles*)   I really don't mind . . .
So what happens, after we present our first mix? *This is what
they do.*
Not just for cost reasons − but because blandness is deemed
essential, OUT go the mushrooms, except for the dreary
button sort of course! Out go the courgettes, cut! Out go the
broccoli and aubergine, cut! And of course out go the
Jerusalem artichokes, *absolutely cut.*
The mix is reduced to something coarse and uninteresting,

and naturally now very closely resembles other products on the market.

He has tossed all the other vegetables back into bag leaving just three remaining.

I just want you to taste . . .

He has produced three mugs and is filling them with granules, and from a thermos hot water.

These are some of the remaining granules, of our first effort.

Clare   Like gold-dust now, I expect.

Boulton   Absolutely. (*Pouring hot water into mugs.*) You see I came prepared. It is hot I hope, but not too hot. Please drink.

Clare   Drink?

Boulton   Please – just a taste . . . to see the difference.

Clare   It's like the Pepsi challenge. (*She takes a small sip.*) Yes, that is nice, *genuinely* nice.

Mrs Trevel   That is good, yes. Really quite rich, pungent.

Clare   And this? – (*She tastes the other.*) Yes . . . the difference is very marked, pretty huge in fact. (*Genuine.*) That's a shame.

Boulton   We are unanimous then. (*To* **Mrs Trevel**.) If you could leave us now please, thank you.

Mrs Trevel (*as if she's been expecting this*)   Yes. Of course.

She exits. Silence. **Clare** *takes another sip, not knowing what* **Mr Boulton** *wants.*

Boulton (*smiles*)   I don't suppose you've had the tragedy of a Ready Cooked Meal demonstrated to you before . . . !

Clare   No. (*She smiles.*) That's certainly never happened before.

Boulton   I know it's something that you would never, ever think of buying yourself –

Clare   Don't be so sure, you haven't seen my cooking . . . !
Anyway I'll certainly walk around the supermarket with a
different perspective now, see the passion that is coming off
the shelves —

Boulton   I'm glad you said that. (*Slight pause.*) Because
being a bright person, you probably spotted what I'm about
to say.

Slight pause.

Clare (*watching him*)   I don't think so . . .

Boulton   When you and Leo are together here you *do* find it
comic, my work, don't you? Laugh together about it, I know
that's what goes on. Or went on.

Clare   No, Mr Boulton. That certainly did not go on here.

Boulton   I know that's what took place. I don't blame you
. . . but I *know*.

Clare   I can assure you, Leo and I do not sit around
laughing at your work. That is a total misconception, if I
may say so, of what goes on here. I do not spend my time, it
doesn't matter which child is in here, I do *not* discuss their
parents' work, of course I don't.

Boulton   Excuse me, but whether it was overt or not, I
know you DID. (*Serious, but not angry.*) *I know that's what went
on.* I can see . . .

Pause.

Clare   Well, if somehow, and I promise you it was
inadvertent, if somehow I gave that impression to Leo, then I
am truly sorry. But I don't see how that could have
happened, because it's not what I feel. (*Looking at him.*) The
idea of taking time, to make something better, and different
. . . not just settling for being like all the other products. Of
course I understand that.

Slight pause. **Boulton** *leaps up.*

Boulton   That will do. That is fine by me . . . ! And please,
keep the drink. (*He laughs.*) No, I would like you to!

He gathers his possessions together.

I'm pleased with Leo's progress . . . no doubt it will
continue.
And I know you don't need telling how much I care about
him. (*He moves.*)
And I'm glad to have had the chance to demonstrate
something – however eccentric it may have seemed. It was
important. At least to me.

He moves again.

Now I must get going – the car – the meter's running (*He
laughs.*) as usual, my fear of wardens!

Clare   Mr Boulton –

Boulton   No, it's fine. I am satisfied. That is all I wanted
from you. I needed to show you – and for you to say what you
did.

He moves to exit.

That's perfect.

He exits.

Clare *looks after him for a moment. She is affected by the encounter.
She smiles.*

Clare (*calls*)   Gina . . . could you come in here please.

In the moment before **Gina** *enters,* **Clare** *sips the meal in a cup, again
struck by how good it is.*

Is Mrs Trevel still here – or has she gone?

Gina   Oh yes, she's still here, very much so.

Clare   Yes. (*Slight laugh.*) I thought that was hoping too
much. Could you ask her to step in then.

Gina   Of course. Richard Mellinger is here, by the way.
His second rescheduled appointment.

Clare   I know. (*She smiles.*) Don't worry, I'll only be a
moment doing this.

Gina (*quiet*)   I wasn't worrying . . .

Gina *exits.* **Clare** *sweeps her desk clear of the remaining spilt granules.*

Mrs Trevel *enters, also holding the mug she got from* **Boulton**.

Mrs Trevel He let me keep mine too! (*She takes a sip.*) And it really is rather good, isn't it – the Meal in a Cup that never was!

Mrs Trevel *sits in front of her.*

Clare Yes . . . (*Staring straight at* **Mrs Trevel**.) I had no idea that you knew Mr Boulton.

Mrs Trevel I don't. It was purely by accident.

Clare By accident? Really?

Mrs Trevel We happened to meet – mutual friends . . .

Clare Now, I want to make myself extremely clear, Mrs Trevel. It would be a very bad move if you tried to go around stirring up the other parents, and it is not something I will tolerate.

Mrs Trevel I'm not stirring anybody. (*She smiles, looking relaxed, summery.*) Although if I was, it's not clear how you would stop it. But that's another matter.

Clare (*very authoritative*) Any grievance you have, any unfinished business, is with me. And should not involve anyone else.
If you *want to continue seeing me* – I advise you to listen to this.

Mrs Trevel Oh, I see. (*She smiles.*) That's your sanction, is it? Good. (*She sips drink.*)

She smiles, relaxed.

But there's really no need for this. I happened to meet him and he told me what was on his mind, that he wanted to clarify the work he did, *to you*. And I said – because I did find his story genuinely interesting – I said I'd come and support him.

Because as you've just seen, it was difficult for him, it wasn't a very normal thing to do . . . (*Self-mocking laugh.*) Though as

you know that's not something I worry about myself! . . .
(*She smiles.*) I'm not exactly an authority on what's normal.

She smiles at **Clare**.

Come on, you can agree with that . . . !

Clare (*calmly*)   And Mr Boulton left reasonably content, I
think. So that's a further reason for him to be left in peace.

Mrs Trevel   You did very well with him, I'm sure. (*She
glances at office toy.*) You've got new office decorations, I see.

Clare   They're my father's, (*Slight smile.*) part of my
inheritance.

She looks at her.

Now – have you been to see any of the colleagues I suggested?
And has George found a new –

Mrs Trevel   Come on, now don't spoil it. (*She smiles.*) You
know I won't talk about that.

Clare   I would like to remind you that the last time you
were here, there was an incident, some violence –

Mrs Trevel   'Some violence' . . . ! Yes, don't worry, I
haven't forgotten. I've already said I'm sorry. (*She laughs.*)
Let's hope there's no need for me to say that again!

Clare   Mrs Trevel, I do urge you –

Mrs Trevel   Please, you've done your duty. I understand.
But do not tell me I need help, OK!

Raising her hand.

And before you say anything, I've actually come here with a
proposal. A compromise, because we don't want to turn into
Punch and Judy, do we? With me keeping on coming at you?

Clare (*watching her carefully*)   No . . .

Mrs Trevel (*smiles*)   And I must be quick, because that
gloriously handsome boy is waiting outside to see you . . . *So*
– if you give me just *some* of George's records, you can fillet

them, like the Government do to their files, you can sanitise them.

Just give me something – then I'll be satisfied.

Clare   I don't think that will be possible.

Mrs Trevel   We could get it all over today.

Gina *enters*.

Gina   Jess is on the line . . . Will you take it?

Clare   Jess? Yes. Absolutely. (*To* **Mrs Trevel**.) If you'll excuse me . . .

Mrs Trevel *gets up*.

Mrs Trevel   Right – shall I come back later to see if you've got anything to give me?

Clare   I don't think I will be here later –

Mrs Trevel   I'll try anyway, then we can all have a good bank holiday . . .

She exits.

Clare *takes the phone call*.

Clare   Yes. Jess? Where are you . . . ? By some gasworks . . . (*Sharp*.) King's Cross? . . . not King's Cross. Where then? . . . the Oval? . . . not there either. Well, I'm not going to spend my time playing guess the gasworks of London. (*Pause*.) So are you going to tell me where you are? . . . You're not. OK.

She sips mug.

No, I'm just drinking something. No, it's not coffee . . . no it's a little complicated. Yes . . . a complicated drink! (*She smiles*.) A farmhouse brew.

Calmly.

You're not coming on Tuesday? . . . why? You never usually ring up to cancel, you going somewhere? You're not. So why is this, Jess? No, I don't think we should move it to some other

time. You're not coming again this summer . . . I see. No . . .
I don't agree.
You'll think about it? . . . Good. Are you alone? No, I just
wondered. OK, call me later today. Yes . . .
Jess – you don't want to tell me anything else? You're sure?
Right.

She rings off.

Richard *has entered half-way through the conversation, he is dressed
in a smart suit, but he is carrying a large rucksack.*

Clare *stares for a second at the phone, deep in thought. Then looks up.*

Clare Richard!

Richard Sorry, I came in, didn't want to miss you.

Clare That's all right. (*She smiles.*) You always look so
smart. What's all this luggage?

Richard You've caught me on a day when I'm in transit.
(*Glancing over his shoulder.*) That woman was here again – I
didn't want her messing things up.

Clare Don't worry, she's gone. I'm free.

Richard But I want –

Gina *enters.*

Clare Yes, Gina? Is something the matter?

Gina *hesitates. Unusually long pause.*

Gina No . . . no.

She moves to door.

No, I'm sorry. It's nothing. (She turns.) By the way I've
decided I'd better stay – in case *she* comes back. (*She exits.*)

Richard Look, I don't want you to say *no*.
I realise there's sort of unofficial rules for seeing ex-clients,
and this would be breaking them – but I want to go *outside*,
for this meeting. Don't say why.

Clare Why? (*She smiles.*) I have to say why . . .

Richard   That Woman may come back for a start . . . ! I
just want it to be less formal, I know I'm setting off all sorts of
psychology beeps and bells . . . 'Why won't he stay here?'
'Why is it so important he moves out of here?'
But say yes . . . It's a lovely day out there . . . SAY YES!

Pause.

Clare (*considering*)   Well, I've got to get my car from under
Marble Arch . . . maybe we can take a taxi over there . . .
and then have a cup of coffee.

Richard   *Let's*! (*Smiles at* **Clare**, *as she hesitates.*) I could
threaten I won't tell you anything unless we do!
Say yes . . . !

Blackout.

Scene Two

The Marble Arch standing upstage.

*Marble Arch, the triumphant Arch is very recognisable, in a rough and
vivid way, made out of cardboard, about four feet high. But it is covered
in McDonald's logos, all over it. In a variety of sizes.*
And arched over the top, like two cherubs, are two McDonald's clowns.

*Hot strong sunlight, the sound of some music drifting from elsewhere in
the park, bare stage apart from the Arch and one normal park rubbish
bin.*

Richard *and* **Clare** *enter.*
Richard *carrying his enormous rucksack.*

Richard   It's too hot for coffee . . . ! How about here?
We'll sit in the sun.

Clare   I think we need a bench, don't we? I'm not really
dressed for lying on the grass . . .

Richard   No, no, I have a surprise, wait! (*He grins.*) I have
a solution.

He drops the rucksack on the ground, and begins slowly to open it.

Clare (*smiles*)   A solution? Sounds interesting . . .

Richard *as he teasingly slowly opens rucksack, glancing around.*

Richard   I used to love it round here as a kid. *Speakers Corner* that was great! Bet you find it interesting what goes on there with your line of work.

Clare   You mean all sorts of different obsessions on show? – Pouring out at full volume! . . . Yes.

She moves.

I remember a man screaming at the top of his voice, that the whole city should be colonised by tropical parrots! – Of course, I haven't been there for years.

Richard   Yeah . . . and there are all the luxury hotels and the cinema with one of the biggest screens in the city – used to dream away afternoons in there. (*He glances over his shoulder.*) At least the old Arch looks the same . . .

Clare   Yes – I suppose it does. (*She laughs.*) Sometimes, when I'm in certain moods – it looks different to me. (*Turning back, indicating rucksack.*) So come on, Richard! . . . What mysterious object is coming out of there?

Richard (*making a flourishing noise*)   Dee dah!

He produces a large quilt, out of the rucksack.

Here we are . . . let me spread it at your feet.

Clare   Do you always carry one around with you?

Richard   And so big. (*Grins.*) You've got to take a good look first – it will surprise you.

He holds up the big quilt. It is a mosaic of airline logos, cut off plastic airline bags, from all over the world, and carefully woven into a quilt. A patchwork of trans-world flying.

(*Smiles.*) So what do you think?

Clare   What do I think?

She pauses, staring at the quilt.

I think you must have clocked up a hell of a lot of air miles. Somehow.

Richard   Certainly. Yeah . . . ! (*He grins.*) So it did surprise you! These are all the airlines I have used – the Logos of the World. With a little cheating of course, here and there . . . I have to admit there are some I haven't used personally, but begged, or stole from people. (*He smiles.*) Or committed murder for.

Pause. He looks at **Clare**.

It's good, isn't it.

Clare (*quiet*)   It's great.

Richard   Step on it, go on . . . You see, you can trace some of my journeys.

Clare   Can I? (*She steps onto the quilt.*) So you really went from America to Africa . . . to Indonesia? Really, Richard? – then down to South America . . . ?

Richard   Yeah, pretty much! During gaps in the course. My girlfriend and I did this . . . the sewing . . . took us ages. And wait a minute.

Clare *about to sit.*

Richard   I want you to look carefully – because there are a couple of clues hidden there, clues to something *interesting* . . . I wonder if you can spot them . . . ?

Clare (*looking for a moment*)   No. (*Puzzled.*) I don't think so . . . do you mean clues to which countries you *really* went to?

Richard   No, no, better than that. (*He grins.*) You'll see it. OK, you can sit on it now. (*He is delving into rucksack.*) Here, is another smaller one!

He puts the small quilt next to the big one, but at a safe distance away from them.

In case we have company – somebody we don't want to get too close! Like that strange lady Mrs Trevel . . . in case she pops up!

Clare   Jesus, I hope not. Why do you say that?

Richard   Because whenever I see you (*He grins.*) she's always there.

He sits on the quilt, but initially there's a considerable distance between him and her.

Now – you've got to admit there couldn't possibly be anything better to sit on in the park, than this!

Clare (*smiles*)   I admit it. (*She looks at the logos.*) Maybe it'll take off of its own accord . . .

Richard *is gazing around him.*

Richard   One moment!

He leaps up, walks upstage, looks at the ground.

It's OK, I just thought I saw something . . .

Clare (*lightly*)   Don't say *you've* found something on the grass . . .

Richard   No. (*Grins coming back to join her.*) Not much of interest over there, just a couple of needles . . . not worth it!

He sits.

Now – just one other thing we desperately need . . .

He delves into the rucksack.

Clare (*laughs*)   Something else . . . coming out of there?

Richard *produces ghetto-blaster.*

Richard   We must have our ghetto-blaster, of course, can't do without that!

Clare   Do we really need that?

Richard   Absolutely! Got to noise pollute the atmosphere, it's essential . . . got to look as if we belong in the park.

He switches on ghetto-blaster.

There are some surprises on here too . . .

The ghetto-blaster begins to play — initially pleasant soft rock, lilting out.

He takes off his jacket, undoes his shirt slightly, beginning to sun himself.

Richard (*grins*)   Now, we could be anywhere in the world!

Pause, he looks at **Clare**.

Tell me.

Clare   Tell you what?

Richard   Tell me, when other old kids come back to see you —

Clare   Yes?

Richard   How are they . . . ? How do they treat you?

Clare   Well . . . Some of them don't look me in the eye. They smile, but they look everywhere except at me. Some kids seem to stoop, like they're trying to rediscover their original size, squeeze back into their old bodies — and others are very loud and confident . . . 'How are you, you old thing! Still at it!' Behave as if they're fifty-year-olds.

Slight pause.

Of course I don't see that many 'old kids', not after a gap of six years.

Richard (*moves slightly closer*)   And what about the ones that were really special?

Clare   'Special' . . . ? (*Watching* **Richard** *closely*.) I can't afford to let any of them be really special.

Richard   Can't you? (*Slight pause.*) Of course you can't.

Pause, he is staring at her.

What . . . if they became famous actors or something?

Clare (*lightly*)   Well . . . I haven't been doing this long enough for that to happen. If you do it for thirty years — you may see children you knew become Top Politicians. And then each time you watch them on TV, all you can think of is them screaming at you 'you terrible, disgusting, evil, old bag!'

Richard   Yeah, I bet . . . (*Looking at her.*) that would be good! (*Slight pause.*) You know when I see somebody doing *your* job on TV or whatever, they *always* look like they've got a poker stuck up their arse – (*Turns to look at her.*) but you, you never do.

Clare (*laughs*)   Thanks, Richard!

Richard *leaning closer.*

Richard   What do you think I liked best about you . . . ? – you won't guess this – (*Slight pause.*) You never EVER used the word 'Skills', learning SKILLS, social SKILLS, lying SKILLS.

Clare (*laughing*)   Well, you were good at so many things, Richard.

Richard (*grins*)   Fuck 'Skills', I say.

Clare *watching him closely.*

The sound suddenly changes on the ghetto-blaster, the music stops, the sound of aircraft noise and nothing else, on the tape.

Clare (*startled looking at the ghetto-blaster*)   What's that? What's happened?

Richard   You've guessed, haven't you?

Clare   Guessed what?

Richard   About my time away. *You know.*

Slight pause.

Clare   Well, I know, maybe, it wasn't entirely happy.

Richard (*grins*)   You've guessed, that it was a nightmare, a disaster . . . a catastrophe.

Clare   Come on now, Richard –

Richard   No, no, it was interesting too! I spent a lot of my time in Airports . . .

Clare (*glancing across quilt*)   As I can see –

Richard   I called it Surfing the Terminals . . .

People are really nervous in airports not just from *fear of flying*, but they're setting out on a business trip that may change their life! Or a holiday which means a great deal to them, or you find them marooned because nobody has turned up to meet them –

Clare   And it's easy to get to know them . . . ?

Richard   Yeah! That's right, strike up an acquaintance! You know what's coming, don't you . . . ?
It's simple to get invited for a drink, or a HOLIDAY even!
. . . Get *Money*, of course . . . *Sex* – yeah – often . . .
Sometimes all those things in one hit!

And then on the plane it's easy to meet others – if necessary
. . . see them struggling with their laptops, tap tapping away
– suddenly not able to make them do what they want . . . you lean over, 'Can I be of help?' a look of such relief in their eyes . . .

I've done the airports of the world, Miss Attwood, I've seen many things.

Pause.

Clare   When did you leave the course, Richard?

Richard   I stuck it for five weeks – then I got the next flight out. And I tried to keep flying west – beat the clock.

I *have skills*, many skills of course, computing skills, all sorts, but there was nowhere I really wanted to land. *Nowhere*.

Clare   Well, Richard – I used to feel like that, at nineteen. I'm old enough to have been half a hippy, and done half the trail . . .

Richard (*loud*)   Don't give me that – don't you dare give me that!

Clare *very startled*.

Richard   Because *this is not the same*.

Clare   And why not?

Richard   Because – BECAUSE – everywhere I went, if it was on a plane, a little plane in South America, or if it was in an airport lounge, with those horrible metal tellies, they have, with those newsreaders that look exactly the same in each city of the world . . .
Absolutely everywhere I was – *I thought of you*.

I saw your face. I smelt you. I saw you.

Clare   Richard – you're exaggerating now, and you know it. You did *not* spend nearly six years thinking of me, that is not the truth.

Richard   Will you listen – I saw *you*, I saw your eyes, you looked at me from buses in New York, you looked at me from little cars in Mexico, I saw you.

He looks across at her.

And now you're this close . . .

He looks down.

You missed it, didn't you? – you see on the quilt . . . *the clues.* There is a 'C' and an 'A' there . . . (*Showing her on the quilt.*) and a whole 'Clare' there. You're all over here . . .

Clare (*looking down*)   Yes. But you could have put those there yesterday . . .

She suddenly looks up. A second later she abruptly gets up.

Jesus – what's the time?
Good God, it's twenty to four! Excuse me . . . (*She picks up her bag which is entangled in his legs.*) I *can't* have missed it!

She is pacing, scrabbling in her bag.

That's just not possible!

Richard   Missed what, what are you talking about?

Clare (*searching urgently through her bag*)   I've got to find the brochure – the programme with the times on . . . Where is it? Maybe he was on at 4.15 not 3.15.

She finds the programme tearing through the pages.

Make it 4.15 *please* . . . ! Where are we?

Clare   The Japanese . . . the Canadians . . . Martin
Pender – 15.15. 3.15! (*She moves.*) SHIT!

Richard   What was at 3.15?

Clare   A lecture. A very important presentation – my
partner is giving the most significant address of his career.

Richard   *And you missed it?* Well, you certainly can't have
wanted to be there!

Clare   No – that is not the explanation.
I thought there was more time – I thought it was later! (*She's
scrabbling in her bag again.*) Just got to make sure I've got the
ticket with me, for the conference, didn't leave it in the office.
It *is* extraordinary how it managed to slip my mind. I'll have
to work out how it happened . . . and *Gina* never said
anything.

She moves, searching for the ticket in her bag.

My car is under here, somewhere! In the car park. Right
under where we are luckily! If I've got my ticket, I can make
a dash across London, perhaps they're running late.

Richard   What will he do when he realises you weren't
there? Your partner? Will he be all understanding . . . or will
he pulverise you?

Clare   I've got the ticket! Thank God for that. (*She moves.*)
Right I've got to rush now . . . so we'll see each other another
time –

Richard (*catching hold of her*)   Oh no – you're not going!

Clare   Richard – let go – don't be ridiculous. Let go of me
at once.

Richard   You're not leaving yet.

Holding onto her.

You've broken one of your own rules, you came out with an old client, because you wanted to know the truth, and now you're going to hear it.

Clare   Richard, LET GO OF ME.

Richard *pulls her down onto the quilt, holding her very tight.*

Clare (*very formidable*)   You will let go of me at once, do you hear? Or I will be so angry with you, Richard –

Richard   You will, will you?

He is lying half on top of her, holding her powerfully.

You're alone in the park with me, anything can happen in parks these days. People vanish off the face of the earth – or get raped for hours, and nobody does anything, nobody answers their cries . . .

Clare *fighting back as he holds her.*

Clare   You're not frightening me one bit. You get off me – you're not going to hurt me and you know you're not. (*His face very close to hers.*) This is so unlike you, Richard –

Richard   You don't know what's 'like me'. You don't know what's happening to me any more.
And I *am* hurting you – because you felt you'd done so well with me, the success I was – your success . . . what you'd made me! I could see you glowing with it, your achievement, oh yes! I could see you, so pleased.

And *now*, you look at me. (*Pulling her head round, really hurting her.*) Look at what I'm like now . . .

Clare   You're making it impossible for me to do that. (*Her head being pulled back painfully.*) Stop this, control yourself, Richard. If you do stop it, we can have a proper time together, OK? Let go . . . will you? Let go.

Richard   You won't go? Promise. If I do. You'll stay?

Pause.

Clare   No. (*Slight pause.*) I won't go.

Richard *lessens his grip*, **Clare** *pushes free, she gets up*. **Clare** *is furious*.

Clare Really, Richard! What was that for? What were you trying to show me?

Richard *sitting in the middle of the quilt*.

Richard I know. (*Pause*.) That was stupid . . .

He looks across at her.

But don't go – please.

He begins to cry.

Shit . . . OK, this is obvious, this is an obvious thing to do . . . me crying . . . this isn't good either, but I *am* crying . . .

Clare *turns to look at him*.

Clare (*quiet*) Richard . . .

Richard Please, I need you here – just for now . . . (*Indicating all the logos*.) I'll take you on the journey I made – the whole one. Show you everything that happened.

Moving his hand across the quilt.

Here . . . and here . . .

Pause. He looks up at her.

But *please* don't go.

Blackout.

Scene Three

Gina *standing, tidying*. **Mrs Trevel** *smoking. Sound of rain outside*.

Mrs Trevel I expect you want to be off?

Gina I'm OK . . . don't worry about me.

Mrs Trevel No – Gina, (*Smiles*.) I'm sure nobody has to worry about you.

Gina (*dryly*)   I try to make sure that's the case.

Mrs Trevel   And you do it really well!

She moves, casually.

You could always leave me here, if you wanted. I could mind the shop . . .

Gina   I don't think I'm allowed to do that.

Mrs Trevel   No . . . (*She smiles.*) Maybe you're right. Leaving me alone with the files on all the children and the parents – might be a wrong move! Yes . . . There's a chance I'd go tearing through them, while everybody was out . . . read all the secrets.

Mrs Trevel *laughs.*

Gina   What's the matter? What's funny?

Mrs Trevel   No, I was just thinking, I could ring round all the other parents 'come on over right now . . . find out what our kids really think of us . . . I've got the keys!' (*She giggles.*) Miss Attwood would come back, and find all these guilty looking couples, turning over her office.

Gina (*slight laugh*)   That wouldn't go down very well, no.

Pause. **Mrs Trevel** *looks at* **Gina**.

Mrs Trevel   I expect *you* hear a lot as the children wait out here, 'My mum thinks this', 'My dad won't let me do that!' . . . Heard anything particularly interesting recently?

Gina   I can't comment on that. You must realise.

Mrs Trevel   Yes, of course. (*Slight pause.*) Do you ever comment, Gina? On anything?

Gina   When I feel the need.

Mrs Trevel (*laughs*)   That's a marvellous gift to have, not to comment! I must take lessons from you, Gina – not commenting is something I find hard to do!

Martin *enters.*

Gina   Hello, Mr Pender.

Martin *doesn't react.*

Gina   Was it OK?

Mrs Trevel   Have you done your lecture?

Gina   Are you pleased? How did it go?

Martin   Fine . . . (*Moving around, very subdued.*) It went well, very well.

Gina   That's good, isn't it?

Mrs Trevel   Is Miss Attwood with you?

Martin   No – she isn't. (*Slight pause.*) I'm not sure she came.

Gina   She didn't go?!

Martin   She didn't attend, no. Not to my knowledge.

Mrs Trevel   Something must have come up.

Martin   Obviously –
It was a big success though. The jokes worked – and the image of this fat ungainly vehicle, bringing a whole city to a halt, *buggering* it up completely, that came across very clearly, I think.

Mrs Trevel   Good. I wish I'd heard it. It was something that needed to be said, and now it can't be contradicted.

Martin   Yes. And I did that. But . . . (*He pauses.*) But just after I finished, I discovered something. (*He stops.*)

Mrs Trevel   You discovered what?

Martin   No, it can wait.

Mrs Trevel   Tell me, I'm interested.

Martin   I discovered the most unexpected thing – a German academic came up to me, congratulated me, then said (*Momentary pause.*) HE'D just written a book about the METROBUS too. And it is to be published next week!

Mrs Trevel   A German . . . ! Written a book about the Metrobus?!

Gina   That's extraordinary.

Martin   It is! It's ridiculous! I said to him it's going to be published just in German, surely? And he said . . . 'Oh no, there's already an English translation, it comes out in *Britain* next week . . . Very good publisher!' (*He moves.*)
He said he'd written it to demonstrate how *not to do things* — for the Transport Planners of the World!

Mrs Trevel (*genuine*)   That is such bad luck . . . It must be really maddening for you.

Martin (*quiet*)   Maddening . . . I mustn't think like that (*He moves.*) I must try to stay calm . . . consider the implications.

Clare *enters. Her hair is slightly wet and rather untidy.*

Clare   Hello. (*Then seeing* **Mrs Trevel**.) Oh, and Mrs Trevel.

She moves over to **Martin**, *her mood preoccupied.*

I'm sorry, darling — something happened, I just *couldn't* be there.

Martin   You couldn't make it?

Clare   No.

Mrs Trevel   We'll withdraw. I think. That would be best. *I* can wait to be dealt with.

Clare (*half under her breath*)   I'm sure you can.

Mrs Trevel *turns at exit with* **Gina**.

Mrs Trevel (*to* **Clare**)   Are you all right?

Clare   All right . . . ? Yes. It's just raining out there. I walked, I didn't have an umbrella.

Mrs Trevel   You walked? Where from?

Clare *slight hesitation.*

Clare   From Marble Arch. I'm fine.

Mrs Trevel *and* **Gina** *exit.*

Clare (*touching* **Martin**)   I'm sorry, darling. There was a problem I had to deal with, somebody who used to come here.

Martin   Really? . . . (*Pause. He moves.*) Well, you missed something. It was great.

Clare   I'm sure – (*Affectionate.*) Did they make a recording of it? (*She smiles.*) Or can you do it again just for me – a private showing.

Martin   But there's something worse, worse than you missing it.

Clare   What?

Pause. **Martin** *paces, his anger erupting now he's alone with* **Clare**.

Martin   I have been beaten – BEATEN, by some fucking German academic, he's written a book too, on the same subject!

Clare   Does that matter?

Martin   OF COURSE IT MATTERS! You really think there's space for *two books* on the bloody METROBUS – of course there fucking isn't.

He paces absolutely furious.

I mean the bloody bus has been there since 1978, the fucking Leyland Titan. There could have been a book any time, but *nobody* thought to write it. and *now* suddenly there are two in the same fucking month! It's a disaster . . .

He moves.

I mean it would be incredibly funny if it happened to somebody else. (*He turns.*) Wouldn't it . . . ?
(*Pause, sarcastic laugh.*) I was such a fool – not to realise I should have written about the Trams of Frankfurt! I was crazy . . . !

Clare *watches*.

Clare   Martin, the work is what matters. *Remember* . . . ?

Martin   That's shit. What does that mean? (*Straight at her, very forcible.*) Tell me what that means? Come on.

Clare (*surprised by his tone*)   It means the work is good . . . and that'll be recognised, and anyway it's worth doing for it's own sake –

Martin   That is such *rubbish* . . . If I ever believed that, I don't now . . . ! It couldn't have been made any clearer could it – the true idiocy of that position – than it was today!

Clare (*startled*)   The idiocy . . . ?

Martin   Clare – I've just seen four years work go down the tubes – I've been whipped.
Timing is everything now – nothing else matters.
Nothing.
(*Loud, as he moves away.*) And don't tell me I'm wrong . . .

Pause, much quieter.

Jesus! I never expected this . . .

Clare   But the work is still there, it hasn't suddenly evaporated. That's not what's happened . . .

Martin   No?

Clare   The detail and the research are terrific. What does it matter if there's another book?

Martin   Stop saying that for Christ's sake. (*Slight pause.*) You know that idiotic woman out there was more sympathetic!

Clare (*quiet*)   I bet . . .

Martin (*suddenly*)   Get rid of her. She's always lurking around now, isn't she? Deal with her once and for all. Then we can talk . . .

Clare   Right, yes, that probably is best. Get her out of our lives.

Martin (*sharp*)   Or do you want me to – ?

Clare   No, no. I'll deal with it, (*She moves.*) it'll be settled.

Martin I'm fetching her now . . . (*As he leaves.*) Make a job of it.

Clare *alone*.

Clare (*sharp*) Make a job of it . . .

Mrs Trevel *enters*.

Mrs Trevel Ready for me?

Slight pause.

Clare I think so . . .

Mrs Trevel (*laughs*) Nearly said something else, didn't you? (*Watching* **Clare**.)
You missed his lecture, your partner. How did that happen?

Clare I had some unexpected business to attend to.

Mrs Trevel I see. (*Lights cigarette.*) Right now, what's the agenda? – Get rid of the crazy lady? For good. Is that right?

Clare *looks up startled*.

Mrs Trevel (*smiles*) You should be able to do that . . .
easy.

Gina *enters with file*.

Gina George Trevel's file.

Clare (*surprised*) Gina, thank you – before I'd even asked for it!

Gina Mrs Trevel suggested you might need it.

Clare Right. (**Gina** *moving to go*.) No word from Jess?

Gina No. (*She exits.*)

Clare *with George's file in front of her, opens it*.

Clare So . . . you want something from here? One piece of paper – and you'll be satisfied?

Mrs Trevel Yes.

Clare Does that include this? – (*Holding up one sheet.*) Your son's birthday, height, weight and school?

Mrs Trevel   Maybe you could look just a little further.
(*Watching her carefully*.)
Are you allowed to use the word freaky?

Clare (*looking up startled*)   What?

Mrs Trevel   I had a young nanny looking after George,
everything was, (*She mimics*.) 'That's Freaky!' I supposed in
your job, you're not allowed to comment all the time 'That's
really freaky!' – Not very scientific.

Smiles, reaching in her bag.

Anyway I'm just warning you, you may find this really
freaky . . .

Clare   And what is in there?

Mrs Trevel   Aha, the other file – *My* File.
Don't look like that! (*She laughs*.) What's the ex-index
compiler up to now?

She produces piece of paper.

This is simple – you know broadsheet newspapers often run a
series of articles from members of the public, 'The Worst
Time of My Life' – that sort of thing? Well, there is a new
series – 'The Worst Experience with My Child'.
And *I've* done one – about you and I.
And my entry has been accepted. (*She lays it down in front of
her*.)
And it appears on Monday.

Clare *facing her.*

Clare   Is that a very wise thing to do, Mrs Trevel? Have
you had a lawyer look at it?

Mrs Trevel   All Names are Changed of course, as they
say.

Opening sheet of paper.

But here *you* are.

She looks up.

Who goes first? (*Without waiting for a reply.*) Me? OK . . .
'The first time I saw her, a handsome confident woman,
polite but formidable, and so very much in control – one of
the most self-possessed people I've ever met.'

Mrs Trevel *looks at* **Clare**.

Clare (*calmly*)   But she made you feel extremely lucky to be
allowed time with her – even though you were paying for it.
Is that what it says? Just guessing.

Mrs Trevel   I'm afraid it's not quite as tame as that.
'A fatal mixture of complacency and arrogance' – that's
what it says down here!

She looks up at **Clare**.

'As I moved nearer to her I realise we're about the same age.
Soon I work out we're both grammar school girls, both from
lower-middle-class families, though of course *she* assumes
I'm from a much posher background – both growing up in
unfashionable parts of London, glorious Acton and Hendon
respectively.' I like that bit . . .
'We probably both had our first sexual experiences about the
same time – maybe even shared the same taste in boyfriends,
tall gangling types, certainly we liked the same music . . .

Slight pause.

'*Now we couldn't be more different.*'

She looks up.

What does yours say?

Clare (*watching her very closely*)   It's not as colourful, I'm
afraid, it's cold and factual.

Mrs Trevel   Cold is good.

Clare (*staring at file*)   'George's mother is very determined
to get results . . . highly motivated for her child.'

Mrs Trevel   I love that, 'highly motivated'.

Clare   'Her previous employment shows up in a habit of
amassed random pieces of information.' (**Mrs Trevel**

clucking in agreement.) 'But currently she is unemployed, her
main focus very much her home life –'

Mrs Trevel (*suddenly very animated*)   Why don't you say
Housewife. I want to be that – officially. I'm proud to be an
'Ordinary Housewife', it's such a great phrase. You should
dare to call me that. OK!

Slight pause.

Clare (*giving her a couple of pages*)   Here, have those. (*As* **Mrs
Trevel** *looks at them.*) Mrs Trevel, did you write this article,
and get it published, purely *for this moment*, so you can have a
kind of 'duel'?

Mrs Trevel (*calmly*)   Yes. Do you want some fruit? (*She
produces some peaches from her bag. Amused smile, glancing at pages.*)
You're right, this is bland, isn't it? (*She looks up.*) And mine of
course is going to appear in *print*, in black and white.

Perfectly calm.

You mustn't forget what my real purpose is in all this. It's
what happens to you – remember?

Eating fruit for a moment.

Now shall we get to the really gritty bits?
'SHE is unmistakably a product of late sixties/early seventies
liberalism . . .' No, this isn't it . . . here!
'Despite all her poise – and while paying lip service to the
worries of a middle-class mum like myself – she can't disguise
her basic *contempt*. It is masked, of course, but I can see it.'
'Her real passion is reserved solely for those poor children,
the NHS cases she deals with, those lost disadvantaged souls.
She approaches what she's doing for *me* as purely a form of
car maintenance – just tuning up the kids. Something that
has to be endured, to pay for her real work.'

Pause. **Clare** *moves around stage taking cigarette out of* **Mrs
Trevel**'s *packet.*

Clare   That is ridiculous and simplistic.
I could say, quite calmly, I refute it.

But in fact it's utter shit, *total shit* and that's what it should be called.

Momentary pause. **Mrs Trevel** *watching.*

I clearly wouldn't survive a week in my practice if people thought that about me.
I do not make those judgements.

She moves over to cupboard in wall, begins to produce a series of Jess's models, both small ones and medium ones.

But there's something much more important that you're wrong about. Far more important *to me.*

She tugs at cigarette for a moment, the models in a pile at her feet.

Mrs Trevel   I didn't know you smoked.

Clare   I don't smoke.

She blows smoke.

I see children – all the time –

Mrs Trevel   Of course. I know –

Clare   – from all sorts of backgrounds. The children of famous novelists and members of the SAS, children of taxi drivers, of traffic wardens with their peculiar new uniforms, and one kid whose father is a pest controller.

She moves.

I have to get to know them, and especially their inner worlds. Have to be able to enter their imaginations – see the world through their eyes . . .
And what you said is *totally untrue.* It's garbage.

Mrs Trevel   Which particular piece of garbage of mine did you have in mind?

Clare   The story about George – when he asked you, 'Am I being targeted correctly, Mummy, towards the right market?' That is *not* how kids see themselves, or see the world now, none of them, not even your son. They do not feel there's such a *rush.*
That is an adult fantasy – a myth.

Mrs Trevel That's what you're calling it?

Clare *Yes*. Just like that other myth – that KIDS CAN'T
CONCENTRATE any more, only for a couple of minutes at
a time, because of TV, MTV, computer games . . .
everything has to be images, and flicking channels, that is
such a lie too!

Mrs Trevel You *want* to believe it's a lie –

Clare *No* – that is not what I find. From the kids. It's not
what happens here. And yet it gets recycled again and again
– 'books will be dead within five years' – it's absolute crap.

Mrs Trevel (*smoking*) So I'm recycling myths, am I?

Clare Kids' imaginations are just as vivid, just as
anarchic, as ever, maybe more. (*Indicating models.*) Look at
these, the work of a thirteen-year-old girl.

She stands them up across stage.

She started with a fragment of the Houses of Parliament,
then she moved on to this great version of the Albert Hall!
. . . a sort of super biscuit tin, whose top rolls off – with these
strange rather sinister black lozenges inside – Christ knows
what those are meant to be!
The whole city is here – though there's a particular bias
towards South Kensington for some reason!
Harrods oozing as you can see . . . a very spiky, dangerous
Albert Memorial . . .

Mrs Trevel *moving among models.*

Clare Just think of the amount of time and concentration
that's gone into these! Hours and hours, to create her vision
of the city.

Mrs Trevel They're great. Strange . . . but great. You
should open it to the public, a model city on your roof! (*She
looks up.*) You must find her a really interesting case.

Clare Yes, she is, I'll admit that. She does all this work for
me, but she will do nothing at school.

Mrs Trevel This is Jess?

Clare   Yes.

Mrs Trevel   The one you're waiting to hear from? I can see why.

She kneels down centre stage, among the models, to look at them more closely.

They're haunting – a sort of two-finger salute, a fuck-you sign, to anybody who looks at them. (**Clare** *turning in surprise*.) And here's the American influence . . . how we half embrace it and half hate it. And they all look uninhabited, don't they?

Picks one up.

Is this what's happening to the city? Nobody knows what the centre of cities will look like, do they? – when everybody's work patterns change.
Somebody said, on the radio, 'Oh, the inner cities will be regenerated by the Entertainment Industry!' What crap that is!

Clare   Yes, that is.

Mrs Trevel   I'd like to keep one of these, a very small one, maybe Battersea Power Station. (*She is kneeling among them*.) God preserve me, from *my* children being too *original*.

Clare   What? (*Sharp*.) What did you say?

Mrs Trevel   I said, don't let my children be too original please – they'll never succeed.

Clare   You really think that?

Mrs Trevel   Yes.

Clare   That's a startling thing to say . . . (*Slight pause*.) Never heard somebody say that.

Mrs Trevel *gets up.*

Mrs Trevel   It's really raining now . . . (*Suddenly turning*.) Do I get to hear my child's recording – what he said here?

Clare   No, you do not.

Mrs Trevel   So there *is a* recording? Of George?

Clare   Maybe.

Mrs Trevel (*watching* **Clare**)   What happened at Marble Arch? Something happened to stop you getting to the lecture?

Clare   A boy, who used to come here, got overexcited.

Mrs Trevel   He attacked you?

Pause.

Clare   No, not attacked, no. That's overstating it. He got upset.

Mrs Trevel   Was it that beautiful boy who's always waiting to see you?

Clare   I'm not commenting on that.

Mrs Trevel   It obviously was.

Clare   I told you —

Mrs Trevel   It must have been unpleasant, whoever the boy was. Suddenly all this bile coming out — was it bile? It must have been a shock. (*Slight pause.*) Come on, you can tell me — before they come in . . . Did he bruise you? (*Taking her arm to look,* **Clare** *flinching.*) Jesus . . . ! You're really hurt.

Clare (*obviously in pain*)   No. It's nothing. (*Slight smile.*) You get very used to kids hurling abuse at you in this job. It happens quite a lot.
(*Quiet.*) I just wanted . . . I suspected this individual was not as happy as he made out . . . but I wanted him to be . . . I wanted to be proved wrong.

Pause.

But it was OK. I'm fine . . .

Mrs Trevel   You walked across London in the rain. Even though you were late for everything! And you say it's OK?

Clare Yes. What's more my car was parked right underneath where we were, right below, and yet I walked all the way back.
That must seem a little odd, I admit.

Slight pause. **Clare** *has turned away.*

Mrs Trevel I'll take you back there. To where your car is. I'll give you a lift.

Clare No. That's not necessary.

Mrs Trevel Oh yes, it's easy for me. On my way. We'll go there together.

Clare Thank you, but no –

Mrs Trevel I think you should come.

Clare You can have this. (*Handing rest of file.*) The whole file – I really don't see why not now.

Mrs Trevel *takes file, but doesn't bother to look at it.*

Clare Have you got what you wanted?

Mrs Trevel No. You were right – it's not going to be of any interest to me. (*Looking across.*) That's why you should come.

Gina *enters.*

Clare (*sharp*) Yes, Gina?

Gina (*glancing from one to another*) I just wondered if you needed anything . . . ?

Mrs Trevel Been hovering outside? Don't worry, she's still in one piece.

Clare It's OK, Gina.

Gina Yes . . . (*Glancing at Jess's models.*)

Mrs Trevel We've made a little bit of mess – but you'll forgive that I'm sure. (*She smiles indicating models.*) I don't know yet if I'm going to be allowed to keep one of these or not? You never guessed you might be able to buy me off that way . . . !

She moves.

I'll just get the car . . . OK? Don't worry I've got a mighty umbrella, I'm fine! I'll park right outside, dash in and get you.

Gina   Get who?

Mrs Trevel   Miss Attwood. (*As she exits.*) I'm leaving the front door on the latch . . . that's safe, isn't it?

Mrs Trevel *leaves.* **Gina** *watching her go, apprehensively. She turns.*

Gina   Where are you going with her?

Clare   She's just giving me a lift – back to where I left my car.

Gina *hesitates, doubtful.*

Gina   Right . . .

Clare   Gina? Tell me. (*Pause.*) Tell me what's on your mind.

Gina   No . . . It's OK. It's nothing.

Clare *angry, then restraining herself.*

Pause.

Clare   Is it my imagination – is it paranoia, not something I usually suffer from – or did you remember about Martin's lecture, when I was about to go out with Richard? You guessed that I might have got the time wrong. You came in – and then deliberately didn't remind me.

She looks at **Gina**.

I'm right, aren't I?

Gina   I didn't want to interfere.

Clare   What?

Gina   I wasn't going to interfere.

Clare   WHAT? Come on, Gina! For once, *just once*, give it to me.

Gina (*comes bursting out with it*)   All right – for once – if you
want me to!
It is because I don't understand.

You don't do things how *I* would. Like . . . like . . . I mean,
parents say to you 'I want my child to come twice a week for
the next couple of months, and after that only once a week
because life's busier then.'
And *you* say to them, '*No no* I can't agree to that . . . *I* decide
when he comes, and how many times . . .'

You're giving a service! You *have* to provide a *service*.

If they want your mobile number, then for God's sake you
give it to them!
Because if you don't, they're sure going to go and find
somebody doing your job who will. (*Watching her.*)
You CAN'T disagree with them. *You can't do it like that!* But
you don't seem to have realised!

Clare (*pause*)   Thank you, Gina. (*Slight smile.*) I was right
then to feel a chill of disapproval coming from you.

Gina   And today – OK, you want to hear about today?!
And so I thought, I mustn't intervene. Miss Attwood has her
own agenda. I must let it take its course. She has her own way
of doing things. *That's what happened*!

Clare   Sounds like bullshit to me, Gina. You thought – I'm
going to move on to another job soon, so just let's step back
and watch how things unfold here – see if she comes a
cropper.

Gina   You think it's *bullshit* . . .
OK! And that's true of my whole attitude . . . ?! And you
think you're gloriously free of bullshit, don't you! Well,
maybe you are . . . (*Staring at* **Clare**, *very calm.*) But I know
what's necessary for me . . .

Martin *enters.*

Martin   She's gone! She HAS gone!

Gina   Mr Pender, I think I'm about to be fired . . .

Martin   *Fired*? Why should anybody fire you? Clare, you're not going to, are you?

Gina   Yes. Because she missed your lecture.

Martin   That's no reason for firing anyone . . . !

He moves.

I have a plan now anyway, I've moved on to the next stage . . .
I've been thinking about it out there – it's obvious! I have to discredit and destroy the German's book . . . *undermine* it . . . There's no way it will be as thorough as mine. I hope! I have to go on the offensive.

Gina   That's right. I'm sure that's right. Go for it!

Martin   Blow it out of the water! (*He smiles.*) If you *can* blow buses out of the water . . .

Gina   I bet you can!

Martin   Have to move quickly, shiftily. (*Sharp grin.*) Maybe even get to review it, the German's book, give it a stinker. If I do nothing, obviously, I have lost completely. I've got to make a virtue out of the timing – two books, one of which is shit, one of which is good. I've got to hound him. *Finish* him. (*To* **Clare**.) What do you think?

Clare   It's not your normal, calm way of solving things. Does it have to be that brutal?

Martin   Yes, I think so. Now it has. (*Slight pause.*) Even the world of the old Metrobus has to be brutal . . .

He smiles to himself.

That is the only way . . .

Pulls out notebook, moves, beginning to write.

I just need to make a couple of notes, while these ideas are still fresh . . .

Pause.

Gina   Mrs Trevel is taking Clare off somewhere.

Clare (*turning, looking at* **Gina**) You've never called me that before.

Martin (*writing in notebook*) What, where to?

Clare It's OK – it's just a ride to my car.

Martin Why? – You know she's a rather unbalanced woman, to put it mildly! (*He is writing in his notebook, only half attending.*) You can't trust her at all . . . she wants to cause trouble for you, make you do something – she's trying to provoke you.

Clare Clearly.

Pause. **Martin** *concentrating on his notes.* **Clare** *moves, picking things up putting them in her bag.* **Martin** *looks up.*

Martin What you doing?

Clare Just collecting a few things – it's the only way to see her off.

Martin (*watching things go into her bag*) Your father's ancient office toys! I don't understand.

Gina Don't go with her, it's not a good idea.

Martin (*deep in his notes again*) Get a cab . . . When I finish . . . I've just got a few more thoughts to get down – I'll come with you . . .

Clare No, I *want* to do this.

Martin *looks up, very surprised.*

Martin Clare, I leave you alone with her, to get *rid* of her and looks what happens! Suddenly you're accepting lifts with her! (*Returning to his notes, he has to complete them.*) And *don't* tell me 'you know what you're doing'.

Clare Right. OK, I won't.

She smiles.

Actually, I probably don't.

Mrs Trevel *enters. They look at her.*

Mrs Trevel Ready? Coming?

Blackout.

Scene Four

Clare *standing centre stage, shaking a bottle of pills.*

Clare Leo, on drugs . . .

(*As Leo.*) Sure I've taken a few, Ecstasy, I take that like vitamins. Yeah . . . means nothing to me . . .
So common at my school, they've got a slot machine for it – you walk in, put in fifty pee, out it comes, one tablet. And it helps! Oh yeah . . . *You* try getting through a day at my school without it!

Clare George on drugs . . .

(*As George.*) I find them on the pavement, people miss them completely! But I see them and they're lying there, for free! I collect them, keep them on the window-sill. Next to my money. But I don't take them.

She puts on coat.

Clare Jess . . .

(*As Jess.*) I don't use 'em. Not much. You don't believe me –? I shot up a couple of times. But I don't need them. Mind you, it's better than sex . . .

This boy is rubbing me, big sloppy kisses, suddenly he's between my legs, really rough. Then he turns me round – pushes me against the wall – he can't really do it from behind – he's just clumsy. But my nose is stuck against this poster – and you know what it's for? It's for a fucking lottery. *Not* the National Lottery, that wouldn't be too bad! – But this was ANOTHER LOTTERY – for a bloody garden centre!

Then I'm walking away, really slow and sore, and I'm thinking why don't I start Jess's Official London Walks?!

You know like the Dickens Walks, and the Sherlock Holmes Walks . . . and while I'm thinking this I suddenly take off – no drugs I promise, this *wasn't drugs*.

I'm in the air. I'm like a hang-glider, I'm floating across the roofs of London, I see a film star down there on her roof kissing her dog . . . I see a stand-up comic with his roof-top pool – incredible blue water, with a sunken sculpture in it . . .

And then right below me there's some professional villains, in their big roof-garden, yeah, with among the flowers they've got a mock-up of a security van! – So they can have practice armed raids – while they're sunbathing!

I'm going across all of this.
Past my window, where I live . . . with the mashed potato still on the screen, on those buttocks, except it's going a bit black from all the smoke.

I'm not *stopping* . . . I'm away . . . I'm right away. Away from school. Away from you. You're not going to get me back. YOU'LL NEVER GET ME BACK.

Clare *exits*.

Light changes.

Marble Arch.

The model of Marble Arch turned round so we see its reversed side. The other side of the model is covered in thick dark bristles, with pieces of litter and flotsam caught in it.

Glowing fluorescence along the back wall. And pieces of long metal strands – fragments of an old machine down stage.

Mrs Trevel *enters*.

Mrs Trevel Come on, I'm sure it's this way.

Clare *enters carrying bag*.

Clare I told you we shouldn't come down that walkway. I have *never* been lost before trying to get into an underground car park!

Mrs Trevel We're not lost.

Clare Oh no? Look at this . . . (*Dusty small metal notice on the back wall with an arrow.*) A pathetic little sign pointing to where the old car pound used to be . . . it's a genuinely scary part of the city, isn't it . . .

We're heading straight for some deserted tunnels! We'll find ourselves wandering deeper and deeper in to the bowels of Marble Arch . . .

Mrs Trevel (*glancing around*) There's so much space down here, isn't there? Much more than anybody realises. We're right under where people used to be hung, Tyburn . . .

She looks up.

Murderers, highwaymen, dangling . . . where all the public executions took place.

Clare (*nervous laugh*) Right, well! – On that note, I think I'll find my own way out. Do without you as a guide, thank you!

Mrs Trevel You think you can just leave, like that?

Clare Yes. With any luck.

Mrs Trevel So why didn't you run off before? When we got out of the car? You had the chance . . .

Clare Because I didn't realise you would insist on escorting me down here.

Mrs Trevel (*slight laugh*) Come on, you knew you wouldn't be able to get rid of me that easily.

Quiet, watching **Clare**.

So you've decided – for some reason – to gamble on giving me a little more of your time?

Clare Yes, well, I didn't plan to be alone with you in a subterranean –

She stops by the metal on the ground.

Shit . . . what is this?

Mrs Trevel   Oh, it's only some junk.

Clare   No. *No*, it's not junk.

She bends over it.

It's still recognisable. Just. It's the corpse of a photo booth –
the Automatic Photo Machine. It probably dates from the
sixties when this entire great hole was dug, and all the hotels
were built –

She squats close to the machine.

Yes . . . look, there's even a coil of photos . . . all smudged,
too black to see.

She stares close at innards of machine.

That's so funny –

Mrs Trevel   Funny, why is it funny?

Clare   Because today . . . because of my father's 'effects'
. . . I was thinking of my teenage years. (*She is fascinated by the
remains.*)

Mrs Trevel   *I* used to play in those when I was a kid,
taking photos of myself, making idiotic faces.

Clare   That's right . . . !
I would pile in with my friends, taking delicious,
'sophisticated' photos, with hats . . . ! Or rude *rude* pictures!
Used to go necking inside these – with some spotty boy, the
flash going off! Even had sex in them. Did you do that? (*Looks
across at her.*) No, maybe not . . .

She lifts part of the metal.

They seemed so new and exciting these machines, when they
first hit the streets *so complicated!* . . . (*She laughs.*) The last
word in elaborate technology.
Now it's old and primitive.

Pause. She stares at it.

If there's *one thing*, that is so different, between now and then
– the city seemed REALLY CLEAN. It was very sexy, it was

erotic to come down to the West End, but it never seemed
remotely dangerous.
The *wider* world was dangerous . . . Russia, Red Square,
men in furry hats . . . but *not the city*.

Slight pause. She stares down.

This is a wonderful relic . . .

Mrs Trevel   You see, it *was a lie*.

Clare *turns.*

Mrs Trevel   You *did lie* to me – when you said you didn't
long for the past . . .

Clare   I do *not* long for the past. (*Slight pause.*) You attacked
me FOR THAT!?

She moves.

Is that what's going to happen again?

Mrs Trevel   Why would it happen again?

Clare   I don't know! I keep thinking that's what you're
planning to do. Give me some sort of ritual beating. A new
way of settling things with professionals that have let you
down! Stuff litigation, let's go and beat the shit out of
them . . . ! *Pulp them.*

Mrs Trevel   You came with me expecting to be beaten up?
You really think that's what I'm after?

Clare   I'm not sure . . . But I can think of better places for
it to happen!

Pause.

Let's see anyway –

She takes a small compact tape-recorder out of her bag.

What result this has –

Mrs Trevel   The tapes of George? Is that what you've got?
So you're going to let me hear them after all.

Clare   If people came upon us now, two mature, 'well-dressed women' as they say in crime reports, playing tapes by a decaying photo booth . . . !

Mrs Trevel   To hell with that – play it.

Tape-recorder between them on the ground. **Mrs Trevel** *circling round it.*

Clare   There is a little of Leo first. Mr Boulton's boy.

We hear real kids' voices. **Leo's voice** *first, a high little eleven-year-old. But it is extremely intense, loud, very upset.*

Leo's voice   I don't want . . . I don't want . . . I don't want, I DON'T WANT TO STAY AT SCHOOL. (*He begins to stretch the words out so they have an insistent beat.*) No point . . . *no point don't want* . . . no point.

The tape changes.

Mrs Trevel   There's George – !

George's voice *pipes up boyish middle-class private-school voice.*

George's voice   MY DAD says he's like a monkey with a computer – and he says I'm like an ANGEL with a computer. Well, fuck that . . . ! . . . Do I want to be an angel with a computer? *What am I doing it for?*

He suddenly shouts desperately.

Nobody will tell me! . . . Nobody can tell me . . . Nobody CAN GIVE ME AN ANSWER.

Clare (*trying to reassure*)   A lot of shouting happens in sessions, with many different children. It's not unusual.

Mrs Trevel *listening with her back to* **Clare**. *She is fascinated. She does not seem bothered by the shouting. She seems almost excited.*

Mrs Trevel   Yes. (*Pause. She listens.*) Don't turn it down, turn it, up yes. Go on, turn it up.

George's *shouting is louder, intense.* **Mrs Trevel** *smoking, moving across stage.* **Clare** *is startled by her reaction,* **Mrs Trevel** *turns towards her.*

Clare   What are you smiling for? I was expecting you
might get really angry, when you heard this – upset . . .

Mrs Trevel   No. This is OK . . . I need to hear this. (*As the
little boy's voice continues to shout.*) This is all right.

Suddenly the tape changes to a girl's voice.

Clare   And this is Jess –

Mrs Trevel   No, don't stop it!

Jess's voice   So I bring these, *to you*. And you know what
they're saying? All these models? – what they're 'expressing',
that's what you want to know what they're really really
saying – well, *it's this!*

*She lets out a high-pitched noise, much stranger than the other children
that builds from a hushed sound to a full scream.*

Mrs Trevel (*quiet*)   Christ – it sends a shiver down one . . .

The noise again.

You failed utterly with her, didn't you.

Clare *suddenly switches off the tape. She turns sharply towards* **Mrs
Trevel**. *She is furious.*

Clare   Thank you . . . thank you very much for that!
(*Enraged.*) JESUS . . . !

For one moment she moves towards **Mrs Trevel** *as if about to hit her.
She moves around her.*

I know you're trying to provoke me. 'Berserk Attack on
Loving Parent' – good late addition for your newspaper
article! And get me hounded out of the profession.

She moves clenched, around **Mrs Trevel**. *Resisting. Trying to stop
herself hitting her. After a moment, slight smile.*

Instead maybe I will beat up an ex photo booth . . .

*She stops moving. She kneels by tape-recorder. She lights cigarette. Her
manner still clenched.*

Mrs Trevel   Keep playing that girl. (*She turns.*) Please.
Please do it.

Clare *switches on tape-recorder.*
Jess *is making a weird chanting sound, no longer a full shout,
sometimes it sounds likes she's crying other moments something
stronger, but it is deeply unsettling.* **Clare** *mouths to the sound for a
moment.*

Clare (*quiet*) Oh, Jess . . .

She stares at the sound.

OK OK.

She shakes slightly for a moment, by machine. Silence except for
Jess's voice. **Mrs Trevel** *watching.* **Clare** *clenched up,
crouched. Then she stops* **Jess**.

All right. You have got to me. (*Slight nervous laugh.*) Brought
me to my knees – as you can see! If only for a moment.

You came after me, pushed and pushed.
When you were being blatant and threatening earlier on, it
had very little effect at all.

She looks across at **Mrs Trevel**.

But today – for some reason – you have broken through. It's
very strange, I don't know why . . . but it's like the
professional mask I have to wear is not operating, people can
see inside me – see exactly what I'm really thinking . . .
(*Pause.*) I've become transparent . . . cannot conceal . . .
The funny little father with his pot noodle . . . Richard – *you*.
That's what you've done. I hope it's not a permanent state.

Pause.

It's like I'm made of glass.

Mrs Trevel Push hard enough and things happen.

Clare Jesus – I wouldn't like to be you.

Mrs Trevel Thank you –

Clare But in many ways you're right.
Not, certainly not, about me making crude judgements about
cases. And you're a Luddite, a romantic and a reactionary
about the past . . . but despite – despite . . .

Mrs Trevel   Being crazy?

Clare   No, you're *not* crazy – immensely difficult to handle – a pain in the arse – but not crazy.

Mrs Trevel   I'm not crazy – that's official! (*Staring at* **Clare**.) I think I've got less conventional as I've grown older. Which is interesting . . . And I think I prove that it's possible to be at home all the time, and still *work out what's going on*.

Clare   That terrible remark you made about children not being too original, in a sense that's true . . .

Mrs Trevel   Yes. I know. And I'm right about the world spinning away from us.

Mrs Trevel *switches on* **Jess** *again*.

Clare   Yes . . . (*A particularly haunting sound from* **Jess**.) Shit – (*Quiet*.) What a noise . . .

She turns down the sound of **Jess's voice**.

You're right about a lot of the control, the Professional Control, in many areas, *being fake*.

Jess's *sound continues*. **Clare** *squatting beside it*.

Clare   I am here . . . surrounded by these kids' voices . . . and I'm saying to you – I don't know . . . I DO NOT KNOW.

Jess's voice, *her affecting cries, suddenly interrupted by* **George**, *and then* **Leo**. **George** *crying out 'what is there for me?' A blend of agitated nervous children's voices. The full power of their voices*.

Clare   Nobody knows what the fuck's going to happen. Because it's all changing so fast. People want service and solutions so quickly.

The children's voices running on.

I am already out of date, according to my own secretary!

Mrs Trevel *turns*.

Mrs Trevel   Panic is good.

Clare   What!?

Mrs Trevel   Panic is healthy . . . Panic is good.

Clare   You mean instead of 'Greed is Good' – 'Panic is Good'. Not sure it'll catch on somehow.

Mrs Trevel   Yes . . . Panic is right. The only intelligent reaction . . .

Pause. **Jess's voice**, *the children's voices.*

They can smell *our panic*. The kids.
But they can see we're pretending it's not there at all.
(*Pause.*) That's why George ran away.

Clare   Perhaps . . . He watched very carefully what was going on . . . it is true. (*She laughs quietly.*) If I go round mouthing 'Panic is good', I'll have no clients left within a week. And *Jess* has already gone.

Pause. She smokes.

But maybe they are waiting for us to admit our ignorance. The kids . . . to hear us say we haven't the *faintest idea* how their lives are going to turn out. (*The sound of the children's voices.*) What work will look like . . . what *anything* will look like . . .

Sound of great clang, like metal exits being locked shut.

Clare   Shit – what on earth was that?

Mrs Trevel   Do they close this place?

Clare   They can't close all the exits, can they? We can't be shut in!

Pause.

Mrs Trevel   Got your mobile?

Clare (*laughs for a moment*)   No, I got rid of it.

Mrs Trevel   Wouldn't work down here anyway.

She starts getting things out of her bag, drinks etc.

Don't worry, we'll get out. (*Pause.*) The whole city's moving out there, the bank holiday. And here we are.

Clare (*stretching out*)   People will come, in the rush hour on Tuesday morning to use the car park and pick their way over these two barking looking women, their hair gone white by then probably!

We hear the children's voices again for a moment, a frightening startled sound, then they are quieter.

And I'll emerge up there, in the daylight, to find Gina running my practice probably! And Martin having murdered a German academic! . . . (*She smiles*) If my 'partner' and I ever split up it will be a problem, because I'll be reminded of him each time a bus goes past . . .

Pause.

'Deeply convenient' – that was how you described my relationship, that was a very *lucky* strike, wasn't it? – An accident . . .

Mrs Trevel   You reckon?

Clare   *Yes.* And if it *is* 'deeply convenient', it is probably what I need. (*She smokes, smiles.*) No doubt, the reality is in fact, that Martin and Gina understand the times perfectly – and it is *me* that is hopelessly out of touch!

Pause. She stares up.

By the time we get out . . .

Pause.

Maybe the whole world will have changed *again*, in *one weekend*. New cars . . . new money . . .

Sound of distant guitar strumming music echoing towards them through subterranean space.

Clare   Fuck, what is that now?

Mrs Trevel   The only other person down here.

Clare   A ghostly busker! That would make my day complete, being raped by a demented busker.

Mrs Trevel   I think we can see him off, don't you!

Clare   Yes . . . I suppose we'd seem a pretty terrifying duo.

The sound wafts away. **Mrs Trevel** *has assembled fruit, drinks, etc. from her bag.*

Mrs Trevel   I'm making a little 'nest' here, we can have a picnic . . . we can last out if necessary!
When they found George – in the woods – at last – he'd built himself a rather strange hideaway . . . (*She laughs.*) maybe this is a subconscious copy.

Clare (*watching her*)   And then you'll let me go . . . ?

Mrs Trevel   You're free to walk away any time.

Clare   You know what I mean.

Mrs Trevel   I've already let you go . . .

She glances across.

Play Jess . . . she may not be making such a terrible racket now . . .

We'll let the city get away, let them sit in their three-mile tailbacks above our heads.

Jess's voice. *A softer singing sound. Still unsettling, but less harsh.* **Clare** *listens for a moment.*

Clare   I didn't know this was here. This sound. It's new, she must have played with the tape when I was out of the room . . . (*She blows smoke.*) I don't smoke . . .

Pause.

I'll have to listen to all my tapes again.

Mrs Trevel   Yes, you will.

Clare   See what's hidden on them.

She smokes; her tone calm.

And then Panic . . .

Fade.

Methuen Modern Plays

include work by

Jean Anouilh
John Arden
Margaretta D'Arcy
Peter Barnes
Sebastian Barry
Brendan Behan
Edward Bond
Bertolt Brecht
Howard Brenton
Simon Burke
Jim Cartwright
Caryl Churchill
Noël Coward
Sarah Daniels
Nick Dear
Shelagh Delaney
David Edgar
Dario Fo
Michael Frayn
John Godber
Paul Godfrey
John Guare
Peter Handke
Jonathan Harvey
Iain Heggie
Declan Hughes
Terry Johnson
Barrie Keeffe
Stephen Lowe

Doug Lucie
John McGrath
David Mamet
Patrick Marber
Arthur Miller
Mtwa, Ngema & Simon
Tom Murphy
Phyllis Nagy
Peter Nichols
Joseph O'Connor
Joe Orton
Louise Page
Luigi Pirandello
Stephen Poliakoff
Franca Rame
Philip Ridley
David Rudkin
Willy Russell
Jean-Paul Sartre
Sam Shepard
Wole Soyinka
C. P. Taylor
Theatre de Complicite
Theatre Workshop
Sue Townsend
Judy Upton
Timberlake Wertenbaker
Victoria Wood

Methuen World Classics

Aeschylus (two volumes)
Jean Anouilh
John Arden (two volumes)
Arden & D'Arcy
Aristophanes (two volumes)
Aristophanes & Menander
Peter Barnes (two volumes)
Brendan Behan
Aphra Behn
Edward Bond (four volumes)
Bertolt Brecht
    (five volumes)
Howard Brenton
    (two volumes)
Büchner
Bulgakov
Calderón
Anton Chekhov
Caryl Churchill
    (two volumes)
Noël Coward (five volumes)
Sarah Daniels (two volumes)
Eduardo De Filippo
David Edgar (three volumes)
Euripides (three volumes)
Dario Fo (two volumes)
Michael Frayn (two volumes)
Max Frisch
Gorky
Harley Granville Barker
    (two volumes)
Henrik Ibsen (six volumes)

Terry Johnson
Lorca (three volumes)
David Mamet
Marivaux
Mustapha Matura
David Mercer (two volumes)
Arthur Miller
    (five volumes)
Anthony Minghella
Molière
Tom Murphy
    (three volumes)
Musset
Peter Nichols (two volumes)
Clifford Odets
Joe Orton
Louise Page
A. W. Pinero
Luigi Pirandello
Stephen Poliakoff
    (two volumes)
Terence Rattigan
Ntozake Shange
Sophocles (two volumes)
Wole Soyinka
David Storey (two volumes)
August Strindberg
    (three volumes)
J. M. Synge
Ramón del Valle-Inclán
Frank Wedekind
Oscar Wilde

New titles also available from Methuen

John Godber
Lucky Sods & Passion Killers
0 413 70170 0

Paul Godfrey
A Bucket of Eels & The Modern Husband
0 413 68830 5

Jonathan Harvey
Boom Bang-A-Bang & Rupert Street Lonely Hearts Club
0 413 70450 5

Judy Upton
Bruises & The Shorewatchers' House
0 413 70430 0

Phyllis Nagy
Weldon Rising & Disappeared
0 413 70150 6